Sherpa Hospitality as a Cure for Frostbite

A personal perspective on the tigers of Himalayan mountaineering

MARK HORRELL

Published by Mountain Footsteps Press

Copyright © 2021 Mark Horrell
www.markhorrell.com
All rights reserved

Paperback edition first published 2022

Except where indicated all photographs
copyright © Mark Horrell

The moral right of Mark Horrell to be identified as the
Author of this work has been asserted by him in accordance
with the Copyright, Designs and Patents Act 1988

ISBN (ebook): 978-1-912748-10-5
ISBN (paperback): 978-1-912748-11-2
ISBN (audiobook): 978-1-912748-12-9

Cover design by Design for Writers
www.designforwriters.com

Sherpa Hospitality as Cure for Frostbite

CONTENTS

Foreword by Alex Roddie	1
Note on the text	4

Part One – Emergence

1	Sherpa hospitality as a cure for frostbite	7
2	An early history of the 8,000m peaks: the Sherpa contribution	12
3	Ten great Sherpa mountaineers	22
4	How to escape from a yeti	34
5	Is it OK for mountaineers to miss a puja?	37
6	*Nawang Gombu: Heart of a Tiger* – a review	41
7	Following the Everesters	47

Part Two – Conflict

8	All you need to know about the Everest fist fight	57
9	A tribute to Sherpas, the tigers of the snow	60
10	Expedition dispatch: the Sherpa sacrifice	71
11	Lhotse 2014: the world's most expensive Everest Base Camp trek	76
12	The Everest Base Camp summit meeting: an eyewitness account	95
13	Leo Houlding does his bit for the Sherpas	104

14	The cod science of Everest hate	112
15	My review of *Sherpa – Trouble on Everest*	120
16	Everest's deadliest day – debating Everest's future	130

Part Three – Triumph

17	On summit certificates, liaison officers and funny mountaineering rules	143
18	Are western operators right to complain about cheap Nepali operators on Everest?	149
19	In memory of Chongba Sherpa of Tate, a high-altitude superstar	159
20	Nirmal Purja's ascent of all fourteen 8,000m peaks: why is it controversial?	164
21	Is the first winter ascent of K2 a turning point for Sherpa mountaineers?	173
22	Why Tenzing is the greatest Everest climber	183
	Acknowledgements	189
	Notes	192
	Bibliography	202

FOREWORD

I can remember the first time I came across Mark Horrell's writing. The year was 2010, I was a climbing-obsessed barman living in Glen Coe, and Mark was blogging about expeditions to high, cold places: Cho Oyu, Aconcagua, and more. *Here's a blog worth watching*, I thought, and I added it to my RSS reader. Other blogs have come and gone, but *Footsteps on the Mountain* has always remained.

Ever since those early years, Mark's mountain writing has stood apart for me. At first glance, many of his blog posts seem pretty simple: informal trip reports and expedition dispatches, delivered in a straightforward, easy-going style, with plenty of jokes and light-hearted banter along the way. But it took me a couple of years to realise that there's a lot more to his writing than this.

In 2012, the media was in full-blown attack mode against Everest climbers, with all the familiar tropes: entitled rich commercial climbers, downtrodden noble Sherpas, queues at high altitude, maybe Everest should be closed, things just aren't as good as they used to be in the 1950s. Many well-respected mountain writers amplified these ideas. Meanwhile, Mark Horrell, who had actually climbed Everest that year, provided an alternative perspective and tried to set the record straight by showing what a commercial

1

Everest expedition is really like.

In the years since, I've edited many of Mark's books about his expeditions, and I've seen his writing evolve to tackle those more challenging subjects with a characteristic flair. Although a hint of nuance has crept into the media's coverage of Himalayan climbing since 2012, the old myths remain stubborn – and Mark's dedication to offering alternative perspectives has only grown. So, when he approached me for editorial help with his latest project, aiming to tell the story of how the role of Sherpas has transformed from high-altitude porters to world-class climbers in their own right, I had a hunch that his insights would result in something well worth reading.

It has been a fascinating and rewarding project to work on. *Footsteps on the Mountain* may have provided the raw material, but his blog is more than just a blog, and this is more than just a collection of blog posts. Not many mountain bloggers have consistently written such in-depth and high-quality essays about the subject. The pieces in this collection include historically significant eyewitness accounts of the 2014 Everest Base Camp disaster and its aftermath – which, politically, was every bit as consequential as the disaster itself, and continues to have implications for Sherpas and high-altitude mountaineering in Nepal to this day.

As editor of *Sidetracked* magazine, I see a wide variety of stories about adventure and big mountains cross my desk every day. It's still uncommon to come across stories that truly look beneath the surface to investigate deeper issues while still remaining accessible and humorous in tone. *Sherpa Hospitality as a Cure for Frostbite* achieves this, but it hasn't come out of nowhere – it's a result of many years of work and experience.

Helping Mark to curate and edit this book, drawing

FOREWORD

threads together and working out what to include (and what not to), has been a pleasure and a privilege. Over many years, Mark's personal experiences with Sherpas, the 'tigers of the snow', has given him a worthwhile perspective that he combines with his knowledge of mountaineering history and literature to weave a compelling narrative. This is the story of how Sherpas, long a vital part of western-led climbing expeditions, stood up and took control of their own destiny – but it's a bumpy road, Nepal continues to face many problems, and there are no easy answers.

Alex Roddie, October 2021

NOTE ON THE TEXT

The articles in this collection first appeared in Mark Horrell's *Footsteps on the Mountain* blog. They have been edited slightly from the original to avoid repetition and to help the flow of the story from start to finish. Although each article can be read separately, they are best read in the sequence presented here. The original publication date appears at the top of each article to provide context.

PART ONE

EMERGENCE

1
SHERPA HOSPITALITY AS A CURE FOR FROSTBITE

27 March 2013

'The healing property of alcohol was the last thing we thought of as we submitted to the feasting and hospitality of the Khumbu and Solu Sherpa villages on the way down from Cho Oyu.'
—Herbert Tichy, Himalaya

Mountaineering history is full of stories of heroic ascents that have come at a cost, especially the loss of fingers and toes (or worse) due to frostbite. We understand how to treat frostbite injuries much better now, and mountaineers who suffer severe frostbite during a climb often manage to survive with all their bits intact. But one method of treatment, discovered by a little-known Austrian mountaineer in the 1950s, seems to have been neglected by the medical profession, and it's one that sounds quite appealing.

When the Frenchman Maurice Herzog arrived back at Camp 5 after the first ascent of Annapurna in 1950, his hands were like icicles after losing his gloves during the descent.

SHERPA HOSPITALITY AS A CURE FOR FROSTBITE

His teammate Gaston Rébuffat immediately took him into the tent and began whipping his fingers with a bit of rope and vigorously massaging them in an attempt to get some feeling back. Down at base camp and during the trek out, expedition doctor Jacques Oudot subjected him to a series of agonising novocaine injections, lasting for hours, which caused him to writhe in pain as his climbing partners held him still. Oudot managed to prevent the onset of gangrene, but eventually all of Herzog's fingers and toes had to be amputated.

Nowadays we know that the rope treatment and vigorous massage only aggravate frostbite and make amputation more likely. Standard treatment now is to gradually thaw out frozen body parts by placing them in warm water, or warming them against a teammate's chest, armpit or even crotch (though it's worth noting that the latter can be sensitive to extreme cold – a patient in America recently sued his doctors over a frostbitten penis after they left ice strapped to his member for longer than necessary).

What has not been studied is why Sherpas are often able to withstand severe cold much better than western climbers, and the Austrian Herbert Tichy discovered a possible reason for this by chance in the 1950s.

In 1954 Tichy made the first ascent of 8,201m Cho Oyu, the sixth-highest mountain in the world, with his compatriot Sepp Jöchler and the Sherpa Pasang Dawa Lama. A small, lightweight expedition with only a handful of members, it was an unusual ascent by the standards of the time – very different to the huge siege-style assaults of 8,000m peaks prevalent until then. When Italians made the first ascent of K2 the same year they had a party of 30 mountaineers and scientists and around 16,000kg of equipment. By contrast Tichy, Jöchler and geographer Helmut Heuberger had just 800kg.

SHERPA HOSPITALITY AS A CURE FOR FROSTBITE

Tichy was already suffering from frostbite after diving onto his tent with gloveless hands to prevent it being blown away in a gale. However, when he discovered they were in a race for the summit with a team of Swiss climbers who had appeared on the mountain without a permit, Tichy realised that if he wanted to make the first ascent then he would have to make a bold strike for the top without giving his hands a chance to recover.

They reached the summit on 19 October, but Tichy's hands were severely frostbitten, and he assumed that he would lose fingers. When Indian customs officers inspected his baggage at the border and found it to be missing 180 pairs of socks, which had been in his inventory when he left, they thought he must have sold them and tried to charge duty. With black humour, Tichy held up his frostbitten hands and asked if they wanted to charge duty on his fingers as well.

But when he eventually presented himself for treatment at a clinic back home in Vienna, he was in for a surprise. His doctor looked at the photographs of his hands taken in the Himalayas; then he looked at the hands themselves, and remarked in amazement:

'You should by rights have lost one or two fingers, but I don't think we shall have to operate. Did you use any particular preparation?'

'I had the usual Padutin and Ronicol injections, plus ointment and massage,' Tichy replied.

'I have never seen anything like it in all my long experience of frostbite on the Russian front. Did you keep to any particular diet or regime?'

'Yes,' Tichy admitted, 'on the way down we were either tipsy or completely sozzled for two whole weeks.'

'Well, that's what saved your hands,' the doctor said. 'As you know, alcohol dilates the blood vessels and stimulates the circulation.'

Pasang Dawa Lama is one of the most celebrated of all Sherpas behind Tenzing Norgay, who made the first ascent of Everest. In 1939 Pasang climbed almost to the summit of K2 with the American Fritz Wiessner; his decision to turn around short of the top probably saved both their lives. He lived in the Sherpa capital of Namche Bazaar, and had been promised a bride there if he reached the summit of Cho Oyu. When the team returned to Namche across the Nangpa La pass, they were invited to join the two weeks of Sherpa festivities in Pasang's honour. The *chang* (millet beer) was paid for out of expedition funds, and Tichy said in his book *Himalaya* that they were obliged to 'comport ourselves according to the laws of hospitality'.[1]

Luckily I've never experienced frostbite myself, but perhaps I too have Sherpa hospitality to thank for this. In 2004, the first time I climbed Mera Peak, several of our team – including myself – wore inadequate gloves and suffered mild frostnip after our -30°C summit day. During the ascent, I took my gloves off and discovered that my hands were purple, heading towards black. I was inexperienced then and unfamiliar with the onset of frostnip, the precursor of full-blown frostbite. One of our Sherpas warmed my hands in his own, a teammate gave me some liquid hand warmers to put inside my mitts, and we continued onwards. My boots were also inadequate, and I returned home with a black little toe. Fortunately it recovered soon afterwards, but the tips of my fingers were numb for several weeks; otherwise I was unharmed. Herbert Tichy's doctor will no doubt have told me the reason for this was because the day after our ascent we spent an evening in the Sherpa village of Tangnag, where our hosts insisted on tipping large quantities of San Miguel beer down our throats.

In my opinion, no mountain is worth sacrificing a digit

for – it will always be there to climb another day in different circumstances. The best cure for frostbite is prevention: to be well equipped with good clothing, and to stay in base camp when high winds are battering the summit. On 8,000m peaks, climbing with oxygen helps to circulate blood to the extremities and is one of the best safeguards against frostbite.

But it's nice to know that a few celebratory drinks afterwards don't do any harm either.

Cho Oyu, Tibet, where the Austrian climber Herbert Tichy discovered an intriguing cure for frostbite.

2
AN EARLY HISTORY OF THE 8,000M PEAKS: THE SHERPA CONTRIBUTION

24 February 2016

The Himalayan Tigers

The Solu-Khumbu region of Nepal (popularly known as the Everest region) is the spiritual home of the Sherpas. Originally Tibetans, they probably migrated over the Nangpa La pass and into Nepal in about the 16th century. The name Sherpa means easterner, because they originally came from the Tibetan region of Kham in the east. They were mostly traders who made a secondary living by farming. Unlike Nepalis from the south, they were used to the high desert climate of Tibet and didn't find the high mountain climate of the Solu-Khumbu at all harsh. To them it was a green paradise. The Sherpas made their home in the Khumbu, growing crops on its fertile slopes, and trading salt, wool, grain and cotton with their kinsmen across the Nangpa La in Tibet.

By the early 20th century their migratory traders' lifestyle had taken many of them across the high passes to Darjeeling in north-east India. The surge in Himalayan expeditions in the 1920s and 1930s created a need for reliable staff and supplies, and a handful of notable Himalayan explorers set up the Himalayan Club in 1928. The club was based in Simla in the Himalayan foothills north of Delhi, with local branches all over British India. Its purpose was to assist Himalayan exploration by providing expertise and logistics to climbers and explorers of all nationalities. One of the products of this was a list of reliable Sherpas from Darjeeling who had provided their services to previous expeditions.

The first man to notice the Sherpas' incredible ability in the mountains was a Scottish chemist and climber called Alexander Kellas. Kellas made eight expeditions to the Himalayas between 1909 and 1921. He completed many first ascents of peaks over 6,000m, and made the first ascent of 7,128m Pauhunri in 1911 with two unknown Sherpas. At the time it was the highest mountain that had ever been climbed.

Kellas shunned elaborate large-scale expeditions, and carried out most of his exploration on his own with just a handful of Sherpas in support. He must have had some amazing stories, but unfortunately he wrote little about his mountaineering achievements. He did write more about science, though. He made many observations on the effects of altitude on the human body, and was known as the world's leading authority on high-altitude physiology.

Everest (8,848m)

Sadly, Kellas is best remembered for his unfortunate contribution to George Mallory's 1921 Everest reconnaissance expedition. He had just arrived in Darjeeling from another expedition to climb Kabru in Sikkim. He turned up late and dishevelled to a dinner party hosted by the governor of Bengal in honour of the Everest expedition team. He was ill for the entire journey into Tibet and spent most of it being carried on a litter by porters.

Eighteen days into the journey, he suffered a massive heart attack and died while crossing a high pass. He was buried in a brief ceremony at Kampa Dzong – a tiny semicolon in the Everest story. Mallory and his teammates continued their journey into mountaineering folklore.

For the world's leading expert on high-altitude medicine to die of altitude sickness 18 days into the first ever expedition to climb Everest is a bit like Muhammed Ali slipping on a banana skin and knocking himself unconscious 18 seconds into his Rumble in the Jungle with George Foreman. Kellas deserves better from posterity and Sherpa mountaineers are surely his most enduring legacy.

Following his lead, the British launched many expeditions from Darjeeling and found that the Sherpas, with their background of living in the high mountains and travelling across them, were ideally suited to employ as porters and mountain guides. While they lacked the technical climbing skills of western mountaineers, they were immensely strong and courageous, and the British discovered that with the aid of fixed ropes they were willing and able to carry heavy loads up very difficult terrain. They trusted their employers and cheerfully helped them in their goal of trying to climb the highest mountains without the ambition to summit themselves. While the British took pains to ensure the safety of the Sherpas, mountaineering is a dangerous activity, and it is likely the Sherpas did not realise the risks they were being exposed to.

During the 1922 Everest expedition George Finch and Geoffrey Bruce spent two nights waiting out a storm in their tent at 7,800m high on the north ridge. They were freezing cold and close to exhaustion, and survived by taking it in turns to suck oxygen from a cylinder. Later in the afternoon, there was a break in the weather. At six o'clock, as they were settling in for a second night, they heard voices outside the tent, and six Sherpas appeared bearing flasks of tea. They had climbed 800m up a steep snow slope from their camp on the North Col, and immediately headed back down again. The hot tea was like nectar, and the following day Finch and Bruce climbed to 8,320m before ending their climb – the highest any person had ever been. Next time you order a drink on hotel room service, and a bellboy arrives at your door carrying a tray, remember this story.

For the Sherpas that expedition was to end in tragedy. After two unsuccessful assaults on the summit, on 7 June George Mallory and Howard Somervell set off with 13 Sherpas up the slopes of the North Col Wall. They wanted to make one final attempt before the monsoon arrived and heavy snow made the mountain unclimbable.

They never made it. About halfway up, they heard a loud explosion above them and looked up to see an avalanche bearing down on them. They were swept down the slope in a wave of snow, swimming frantically to keep themselves above the surface. When they came to rest they were able to pull themselves free, but below them they could see that nine Sherpas in two rope parties had been buried alive. They rushed down and were able to pull two of them free of the snow. Seven died.

The Sherpas had trusted the British to lead them safely, but there had been a great deal of fresh snowfall, and Somervell and Mallory knew they had been taking a great risk. Somervell summed up their feelings later.

Only Sherpas and Bhotias killed – why, oh why could not one of us Britishers have shared their fate? I would gladly at that moment have been lying there dead in the snow, if only to give those fine chaps who had survived the feeling that we shared their loss, as we had indeed shared the risk.[2]

Kangchenjunga (8,586m)

The late 1920s and 1930s saw a flurry of expeditions to the 8,000m peaks. In 1929 a young American called Edgar Farmer tried to climb Kangchenjunga illegally and probably died somewhere on the south face. A well-organised German expedition led by Paul Bauer reached 7,400m on the north-east spur later that year before being caught in a five-day storm.

The following year, an international expedition led by the Swiss Gunther Dyhrenfurth made another attempt on Kangchenjunga from the western Nepalese side. Before leaving for India, Dyhrenfurth was contacted by Edgar Farmer's mother, who said that she had seen her son in a dream being held captive at a monastery in the Yalung Valley. Dyhrenfurth promised to look for him, but he didn't say how. Would his team of elite mountaineers storm the monastery with their ice axes and free the poor captive from his evil monastic kidnappers in a daring night-time raid? We will never know, because when they got there the monastery was derelict, and there was no sign of Farmer or his captors. He probably died on the mountain after all.

Dyhrenfurth's team made little progress during the climb. They attempted the north ridge but found it to be an avalanche hell. One of them, Erwin Schneider, was lucky to survive when an ice cliff collapsed and swept him away. Twelve Darjeeling Sherpas were climbing with him, and one of them, Chettan, wasn't so lucky. Chettan's death affected morale. The team abandoned the north ridge and left it for bolder climbers.

K2 (8,611m)

An Italian team led by Prince Luigi Amedeo, Duke of

Abruzzi, made an early attempt on K2 in 1909. The expedition reached about 6,250m on the south-east spur. In the 1930s, two American teams followed in their footsteps. Unlike the Italians, they didn't have any dukes to lead them (apart from Duke Ellington, who probably had to decline the invitation because of a gig).

Their 1938 expedition was led by Charles Houston, who later explored the south side of Everest in 1950 with Bill Tilman. It was a successful expedition. Houston and three experienced climbers – Bob Bates, Bill House and Paul Petzoldt – opened the route up the Abruzzi Spur. House completed a difficult rock pitch now known as House's Chimney, and Petzoldt reached as high as 7,925m.

By contrast the 1939 expedition, led by German-born Fritz Wiessner, who had become a US citizen four years earlier, is not one of high-altitude mountaineering's proudest episodes. While Wiessner was a brilliant and determined climber, the rest of his team weren't; and only one of them, Dudley Wolfe, was prepared to do much climbing above base camp.

That Wiessner and a Sherpa, Pasang Dawa Lama, managed to reach as high as 8,370m is testament to the skill of both climbers. In those days climbing high on an 8,000m peak required strong support from other team members. But Wiessner may as well have been supported by the crew of the *Mary Celeste* for all the help he received from his team.

Wolfe, who wasn't a good enough climber to be attempting a mountain like K2, was left at Camp 8 at 7,700m while Wiessner and Pasang made their summit attempt. When the pair returned to the camp they discovered that nobody had been up to resupply it and Wolfe was dangerously ill. They managed to get him down to Camp 7, but he could go no further, and they left him there while they descended for help.

Camp by camp, Wiessner and Pasang descended and found that everything had been cleared by their teammates in their absence. With nowhere to stop and rest they had to descend all the way to base camp at 5,400m before they could find anyone able to rescue Wolfe.

At Camp 7 Wolfe was a long way from help and deteriorating rapidly. Three valiant Sherpas, Pasang Kikuli, Pasang Kitar and Pintso, set off up the mountain to rescue him, but they were never seen again.

Nanga Parbat (8,125m)

Meanwhile, German mountaineers were also having problems on another 8,000m peak: Nanga Parbat, a mountain where British climber Albert Mummery and two Gurkha officers went missing in 1895.

In 1932 Willy Merkl led a successful reconnaissance, which reached 7,000m on Nanga Parbat's east ridge and remained free from accidents (although one of the team, Rand Herron, fell and died climbing one of the Pyramids of Giza during a short visit to Egypt on the way home).

By contrast the two expeditions to follow, in 1934 and 1937, suffered 26 fatalities between them. The 1934 expedition had already lost one member, Alfred Drexel, to pneumonia, when 16 of them found themselves retreating for their lives from Camp 8 in a storm on 8 July. Karl Herrligkoffer, half-brother of one of the casualties, later said that 'for sheer protracted agony [it] has no parallel in mountaineering history'.[3] The two strongest climbers, Austrians Peter Aschenbrenner and Erwin Schneider, unroped from the party and were safely back in Camp 4 the same day, where they collapsed exhausted. They told those waiting at Camp 4 that their companions would be arriving shortly.

As 1930s accuracy goes, this statement was on a par with Neville Chamberlain saying there was peace for our time and we should get a nice sleep. Moreover, the Austrians knew it. They had skied down, and they will have known that without skis the three Sherpas they had unroped from – Pasang, Nima Dorje and Pinzo Norbu – would be much slower. The three Sherpas made it no further than Camp 7, and spent the night with no food or drink and a single sleeping bag between them. Expedition leader Willy Merkl, Willo Welzenbach, Ulrich Wieland and eight Sherpas hadn't done quite as well as that, and were spending the night in a bivouac somewhere below Camp 8. Nima Norbu died there – the first of many to go. Three of the Sherpas, Ang Tsering, Gaylay and Dakshi, decided to stay there another night while the rest of the team descended. Wieland died a few metres short of Camp 7, where Merkl and Welzenbach spent the night after sending the four Sherpas, Kitar, Pasang Kikuli, Nima Tashi and Da Thundup, on to Camp 6. The four didn't make it to camp, and spent another night out in the open. Unknown to them, Pasang, Nima Dorje and Pinzo Norbu, were sleeping not far away in a snow cave after losing their way in the whiteout. The seven Sherpas met up on the traverse of Rakhiot Peak and continued down together. But Nima Dorje collapsed and died as Da Thundup was helping him down the fixed ropes. A little below them Nima Tashi was also sitting lifeless in the snow. Pinzo Norbu died just as he reached camp. In the late afternoon of 10 July, an exhausted Pasang, Kitar, Pasang Kikuli and Da Thundup reached the relative safety of Camp 4, two days after Aschenbrenner and Schneider had said they would be just a few minutes.

Up above them all was not well. Dakshi had died in the bivouac above Camp 7; Ang Tsering and Gaylay continued their descent on 11 July. They stumbled across Wieland's body as they approached Camp 7, where they found Merkl and Welzenbach clinging onto life. It was clear that Welzenbach was beyond help. Ang Tsering tried to persuade Merkl to leave without him, but Merkl refused. All four stayed in Camp 7 on 12 July until Welzenbach passed away the following night. The three survivors continued the next morning. It was their eighth day without food and sixth without water. It was also Merkl's last. He had severe frostbite in his hands and feet; the two Sherpas had to help him with every step. They stayed another night on the mountain, but the following day Merkl could no longer go on. Ang Tsering continued to try and get help, eventually reaching Camp 4 and safety, but Gaylay stayed with his leader. The pair of them died some time on 15 or 16 July, more than a week into the retreat.

The disaster that struck the German team in 1937 was more straightforward. The British transport officer, Lieutenant Smart of the Gilgit Scouts, descended from Camp 4 with a team of four Balti porters to find Uli Luft preparing to head on up in support.

When Luft arrived at Camp 4 on 18 June he could find no trace of it. The entire thing, tents and men, had disappeared under an avalanche of devastating size, killing 16 people as they slept. Nine of them were Sherpas. It was probably a kinder way to go than Merkl's team in 1934.

Paul Bauer of Kangchenjunga fame had become heavily involved with Adolf Hitler's Reich Sports Ministry. It had now become a matter of Nazi pride that Nanga Parbat should be conquered. Undeterred by the two disasters of 1934 and 1937, he pressed ahead with another expedition in 1938.

They didn't climb any higher than previous expeditions, but they did discover the bodies of Willi Merkl and Gaylay near a feature called the Moor's Head. Gaylay had not left

Merkl's side. His extraordinary self-sacrifice was up there with that of Pasang Kikuli, Pasang Kitar and Pintso on the second American K2 expedition.

The early history of the 8,000m peaks has traditionally been seen as a competition between Europeans and Americans to become the first nation to climb one. However, none of their expeditions could have gone ahead without the help of Sherpas, who often paid for it with their lives.

The history of the 8,000m peaks was driven by western exploration, but the Sherpa contribution should never be forgotten. While initially employed as porters, Sherpas eventually performed so well at high altitude that the best of them became mountaineers in their own right. The Sherpas on the official Himalayan Club list became known as Tigers. Very few western mountaineers have ever climbed an 8,000m peak without their assistance. Fittingly, one of them, Tenzing Norgay, made the first ascent of Everest with Edmund Hillary in 1953.

3
TEN GREAT SHERPA MOUNTAINEERS

19 March 2014

Soon I'll be heading to Lhotse in Nepal for my sixth attempt at an 8,000m peak, and I very much hope my third successful one, although you can never be sure in mountaineering. One thing I do know is that I would stand very little chance of getting up any of them were it not for the dozens of Sherpas who have helped me over the years.

As the Everest season approaches, we will be hearing a lot about the successes of western climbers in the Himalayas over the next few months, but likely very little about the superstars of high-altitude mountaineering who help them to achieve their dreams.

Many of you can probably name all the famous Sherpas you've heard of on one hand. It's time someone rectified this, so here's two hands' worth of the greatest tigers of the snow.

1. Angtharkay

'Outstandingly the best of all the Sherpas I have known ... he was a most loveable person: modest, unselfish and completely sincere,'[4] the mountain explorer Eric Shipton once said of Angtharkay, the first of the great mountaineering *sirdars* (Sherpa leaders), and the one who can be considered the grandfather of them all.

Born and raised in the village of Khunde above Namche Bazaar in the Khumbu region of Nepal, like many Sherpas of the 1920s and 1930s he emigrated to Darjeeling in north-east India in search of work with mountaineering expeditions, which in those days all used Darjeeling as their home base rather than Kathmandu. While on his third major job, the 1933 British Everest expedition, he was recognised by Shipton for his outstanding leadership and strong performance at high altitude. He became Shipton's trusted right-hand man, accompanying him on his mountain reconnaissance expeditions to the Nanda Devi Sanctuary and the Shaksgam region north of K2. He also served as sirdar on three more Everest expeditions.

In 1950 he was sirdar for the French expedition to Annapurna, which became the first to climb an 8,000m peak. He showed great wisdom by turning down his opportunity to be in the summit party with the following immortal line, quoted by Maurice Herzog in his classic book about the expedition:

> *Thank you very much, Bara Sahib, but my feet are beginning to freeze and I prefer to go down to Camp 4.*[5]

Herzog and Louis Lachenal reached the summit, but they had an epic descent. Both lost their toes to frostbite; Herzog lost his fingers as well.

Eric Shipton's 1951 Everest reconnaissance expedition illegally strayed into Tibet while exploring a remote Himalayan valley. Despite travelling mostly by night to avoid detection, there was a nasty incident when they were spotted by a group of Tibetans, who charged towards them brandishing swords and shouting. Shipton was worried about being arrested and thrown into prison – not only because he was carrying a mere 1,200 rupees to purchase their freedom, but because it might jeopardise any future permission to climb in Nepal. But Angtharkay came to the rescue and immediately started shouting back at them.

'I have never known Angtharkay outdone in a shouting match,'[6] Shipton later observed. Twenty minutes later Angtharkay returned with a broad grin, and explained it was going to cost 7 rupees to buy them off (about $20). His anger with the Tibetans had been because they initially demanded 10.

2. Gaylay

His name may elicit playground chuckles, but Gaylay has come to represent something more meaningful: the huge sacrifices Sherpas have made to further the ambitions of their western employers.

He was one of the six Sherpas and three German climbers who died during a horrifying four-day retreat high on Nanga Parbat in 1934. Exhausted and frostbitten, they died one by one in lonely bivouacs as a storm battered them to submission. By the fourth day Gaylay, Ang Tshering and expedition leader Willi Merkl were the only ones left when Merkl said he could go no further. While Ang Tshering went to fetch help, Gaylay stayed with his leader, and neither was seen alive again. Four years later their perfectly preserved bodies were found on the Rakhiot Ridge by another German team. Gaylay had not left Merkl's side.

Of the 248 climbers who have died on Everest by 2014, 87 are Sherpas, who do the lion's share of the dangerous work but share very little of the limelight. Since the very first attempt in 1922, when seven Sherpas died in an avalanche while carrying loads up to the North Col for George Mallory, to the present day, when Mingma Sherpa died in the Khumbu Icefall in 2013 installing fixed ropes and ladders for commercial expedition teams, Sherpas have been the unsung heroes of every expedition. When I stumbled back to high camp exhausted during my 18-hour summit day on Everest in 2012, my Sherpa companion Chongba remained by my side throughout, even though he could have returned hours earlier in good shape had he wanted to.

Gaylay symbolises all of these men, and deserves to be remembered as one of the great Sherpa mountaineers.

3. Tenzing Norgay

The best known of all, Tenzing was the man who brought Sherpas to worldwide attention when he reached the summit of Everest with Edmund Hillary in 1953. But while Hillary had only been climbing in the Himalayas for two years, and in many ways can be regarded as a man who happened to be in the right place at the right time, Tenzing was on his seventh Everest expedition, and his Himalayan mountaineering career had already spanned nearly two decades.

Tenzing was raised in the Khumbu region of Nepal, and moved to Darjeeling as a teenager in search of work. In 1935, Eric Shipton was picking Sherpas for the latest Everest expedition when he noticed a 'Tibetan lad of nineteen, a newcomer, chosen largely because of his attractive grin'.[7] Like Angtharkay, Tenzing was an outstanding organiser and leader of men, and became the trusted sirdar to many expeditions – but he also had another quality that marked him out among his people.

Until Tenzing, Sherpas had been content to carry loads high to give their employers a chance of climbing the mountain, but none of them ever showed any desire to reach the summit themselves. Tenzing was different. His ambition to climb Everest was as great as any western climber's. By the time the Swiss and the British took him to Everest as sirdar in 1952 and 1953, he had become so competent that he was seen as an integral part of the climbing team. The rest is history.

4. Pasang Dawa Lama

The disastrous American expedition to K2 in 1939 is sometimes described as a one-man show by the energetic German-born expedition leader Fritz Wiessner, but this isn't strictly true. When Wiessner reached 8,370m, just 240m below the summit, he wasn't alone. While Wiessner wanted to continue to the summit, it was his companion Pasang Dawa Lama who made the decision to turn around. Pasang's caution probably saved their lives. As they descended exhausted they found that Wiessner's cowardly teammates had systematically stripped their support camps and were preparing to leave the mountain, believing them to be dead.

Pasang eventually had his chance to ascend an 8,000m peak 15 years later, when he made the first ascent of Cho Oyu with the Austrians Herbert Tichy and Sepp Jöchler in 1954. He was back in Namche Bazaar restocking supplies when Tichy and Jöchler discovered that they were not alone on the mountain, and had to make their daring dash for the top – which worsened Tichy's frostbite. Pasang hurried back to join them, ascending 4,250m in three days to join the summit party. As we have seen, he had a special incentive: while back in Namche he struck a bargain with a villager, who offered him the hand of his daughter in marriage and a substantial dowry if he reached the summit.

Later that same year, 1954, Pasang came within a whisker

of making the first ascent of Dhaulagiri with an Argentine team. He bivouacked with his brother Ang Nima and two other team members at 8,000m, just 167m below the summit, but had to descend the following morning due to a snowstorm. Pasang was also a member of the four-man team who made the first ever foray into the Khumbu Icefall during Eric Shipton's 1951 Everest reconnaissance expedition. In 1958 he made the second ascent of Cho Oyu with an Indian team, becoming the first man to ascend the same 8,000m peak twice.

5. Gyalzen Norbu Sherpa

Only three men have been involved in two separate first ascents of 8,000m peaks. Two of them – Hermann Buhl, who climbed Nanga Parbat and Broad Peak, and Kurt Diemberger, who climbed Broad Peak and Dhaulagiri – are world famous. The third, Gyalzen Norbu Sherpa, is virtually unheard of, yet he was the first man in history to climb two 8,000m peaks.

Gyalzen Norbu was sirdar for the French expedition to Makalu in 1955, and one of the support climbers in an astonishingly successful expedition that put nine climbers on the summit over three successive days. He was a member of the second party and the only Sherpa in the climbing team. By the time he went to Manaslu with the Japanese in 1956 his reputation was firmly established, and as well as being sirdar he was one of the two lead climbers. At Camp 5, the expedition doctor Hirokichi Tatsunama fed oxygen to Gyalzen Norbu and Toshio Imanishi through tubes from the adjacent tent. Six climbers supported their summit attempt by carrying tents to Camp 6. Imanishi's shot of Gyalzen Norbu raising his ice axe on the shattered rock tower of Manaslu's summit is one of the great iconic photographs of

Himalayan mountaineering.

6. Nawang Gombu

Nawang Gombu, a nephew of Tenzing Norgay, was sent away to the Rongbuk Monastery in Tibet as a boy to train as a monk. After realising that monastic life wasn't for him, he fled across the Nangpa La back to his family in the Khumbu village of Thame.

In 1952 the Swiss attempted Everest with Tenzing as their sirdar, and Gombu went to Namche to plead with his uncle for a place on his next expedition. When the British came to Everest the following year, the 17-year-old Gombu was granted a place as climbing a Sherpa. Expedition leader John Hunt recalled an incident in the Khumbu Icefall when the two of them were doing a load carry and Gombu noticed that his leader was only carrying one oxygen bottle to his two.

'Why you not have two bottles?' he asked.

Tenzing was furious when he heard about it, but Hunt found the incident very funny. Gombu later did two very important load carries to the South Col in support of the successful first ascent by his uncle and Edmund Hillary. When the Indian government set up the Himalayan Mountaineering Institute (HMI) in Darjeeling as a result of Tenzing's success, Gombu was one of the Sherpas sent to Switzerland to train as an instructor.

Over the next ten years he went on expeditions to Makalu, Cho Oyu and Everest before being chosen to join the American expedition to Everest in 1963. When Jim Whittaker became the first American to climb the world's highest mountain, Gombu stood beside him on the summit. Later that year he was invited to the US to be introduced to President John F. Kennedy. The following year he reached the summit of Nanda Devi, and in 1965 he joined an Indian expedition to Everest and became the first person to climb it twice.

He took over from Tenzing as director of field training at HMI in 1976. He remained in that position for 23 years until his retirement in 1999, an achievement even Sir Alex Ferguson would have been proud of.

7. Pertemba Sherpa

'He seemed at home in any situation in the west, and yet he hadn't lost the traditional values of Sherpa society. He had that combination of twinkling humour, dignity and warmth that is one of the enduring qualities of so many Sherpas.'[8] So said the great pioneering British mountaineer Chris Bonington, who took Pertemba along as his lead climbing Sherpa on a number of expeditions in the 1970s.

Pertemba was one of the first of a new breed of Sherpas who bridged the divide between east and west and moved comfortably among western mountaineers on an equal footing. He was a pupil of Sir Edmund Hillary's first school, in the Khumbu village of Khumjung. In the mid-1960s he moved to Kathmandu to work for the grandfather of trekking in Nepal, Colonel Jimmy Roberts, who had just opened Mountain Travel, the very first trekking agency for western tourists.

Pertemba's first taste of a mountaineering expedition came in 1970 as part of Chris Bonington's team, who made the first ascent of the south face of Annapurna. His climbing skills so impressed his leader that he soon became a climbing Sherpa. When he made his first ascent of Everest in 1975, it was not by the standard south-east ridge, but by a much more technical route up the south-west face, and he reached the summit in overcast conditions with the climbing legend Pete Boardman. He climbed Everest again with a German team in 1979, and again with a Norwegian team in 1985. On this third and final climb he reached the top with his old friend and mentor Chris Bonington.

Pertemba eventually set up his own trekking agency, and climbed further afield in Britain, Switzerland and Alaska. He became a grandee of mountaineering in Nepal, serving as a committee member of Hillary's charity the Himalayan Trust, an executive member of the Nepal Mountaineering Association (NMA), and a member of the Kathmandu Environmental Education Project (KEEP), which educates both westerners and Nepalis on environmental issues.

8. Babu Chiri Sherpa

If Pertemba was one of the first Sherpas to take on western values, Babu Chiri was the first to eat them for breakfast, chew on them and spit them back. He can fairly be described as the very first stunt Sherpa. Every year a handful of westerners turn up at Everest with film crews and down suits emblazoned with sponsors' logos in pursuit of some bizarre stunt they hope will garner media attention, but few of them ever do anything to match the remarkable achievements of Babu Chiri.

As many Sherpas do, he began his expedition life as a porter and moved up the ranks until he achieved his first 8,000m peak summit, Kangchenjunga, at the age of only 23. Summits of Dhaulagiri, Shishapangma and Cho Oyu followed, but it was on Everest that he made his name. He climbed the mountain ten times between 1990 and 2000, and in 1995 became one of the first to climb it twice in a single season. On 20 May 2000 he set off from base camp at 5pm, and was on the summit at 9.56 the following morning, having climbed the mountain in what at the time was a jaw-dropping, lung-squeezing 16 hours 56 minutes. It takes most people four days. This was the first Everest speed ascent and he later said he would have climbed it more quickly had it not been for the blizzard he encountered on the way up.

But in 1999 he completed what was arguably an even more extraordinary achievement. When I reached the summit of Everest myself in 2012, I spent just five minutes there and took a couple of photos, conscious that I still had a long descent ahead of me. In 1999 Babu Chiri took a tent and pitched it on the summit. He spent 21 hours there without bottled oxygen, and sang the national anthem into a radio while it was broadcast live from base camp on Radio Nepal. Take note all those people who think it's significant to make a cell-phone call or a short television interview from the summit.

Who knows what other amazing feats Babu Chiri might have achieved had he not died in bizarre fashion in 2001, when he fell into a crevasse at Camp 2 in the Western Cwm while stepping backwards to take a photograph.

9. Apa Sherpa

For much of his career Apa Sherpa found himself in friendly competition with Ang Rita Sherpa for the record of greatest number of Everest ascents. As the younger man at a time when commercial climbing on Everest was becoming firmly established, it was a competition that Apa Sherpa eventually won. He climbed the mountain nearly every year between 1990 and 2011, and by the time he retired at the age of 51 he had reached the highest point on the planet an incredible 21 times.

More recently Apa Sherpa has become something of an ambassador, raising awareness of climate change in the Himalayas. His last four Everest ascents were part of the Eco

Everest Expedition project. In addition to reaching the summit, the teams also had the more important objective of removing historical debris from the mountain. By 2012 these expeditions had removed 13,500kg of waste from Everest, including 450kg of excrement and a number of dead climbers whose families had requested they be brought down. Thanks to Apa Sherpa and his teammates, Everest is now a much cleaner mountain.

10. Phurba Tashi Sherpa

So far I have only listed Sherpas who either passed away long ago or are now retired. It seems fitting to end with someone who is still climbing in 2014 – and one name stands out.

People who have watched the *Everest: Beyond the Limit* documentaries broadcast by the Discovery Channel (2006–2009) may remember seeing Phurba Tashi berating the figure of exhausted American climber Tim Medvetz as he slumped on a fixed rope on the north-east ridge a few metres short of Everest's summit.

'You are so lazy!' he cried.

This may sound unfair, but Phurba Tashi wasn't being unkind or disrespectful to his client. He knew what a perilous situation they were in; if he didn't get Medvetz moving then he would remain up there. He stayed with him, cajoled him into action, and eventually got him back down the mountain safely.

For many years Phurba Tashi has been the right-hand man of the New Zealander Russell Brice, one of the grandfathers of commercial mountaineering on Everest. Phurba Tashi holds the record for the greatest number of successful ascents of 8,000m peaks – 30 – and last year he equalled Apa Sherpa's record of 21 Everest ascents while climbing with Brice's Himex expedition team. This year (2014) he is very likely to beat it, and even then he won't be finished.[9]

You never conquer a mountain like Everest, but Sherpas like Phurba Tashi seem to have found a way of living in harmony with it so that an ascent every season seems all but guaranteed. They have come a long way since Angtharkay's days in the 1930s, but despite being the superstars of high-altitude mountaineering, a surprisingly high number of Sherpas keep their feet firmly on the ground and maintain their great reputation for cheerfulness, hard work and humility.

4
HOW TO ESCAPE FROM A YETI

24 August 2011

The great Tyrolean mountaineer Reinhold Messner famously claimed to have seen a yeti when he was camping alone in a clearing in Tibet in 1986. Whatever it was, it moved adeptly on two legs and was too big to be a man. Not surprisingly, people accused him of being bonkers when he returned home and described the encounter, and he spent a good few years trying to back up his claim. Among his many books about climbing all of the world's 8,000m peaks is the curiosity *My Quest for the Yeti*, which documents his search to uncover the truth about the elusive Himalayan beast. He eventually found another one – in Lhasa Zoo of all places. The Tibetans called it a *chemo*, and he concluded that it was some unknown species of brown bear.

Frank Smythe devoted a whole chapter of his book *The Valley of Flowers* – which is about a mountaineering expedition to Garhwal in the Indian Himalayas in 1937 – to the Abominable Snowman. He described seeing the footprints of a five-toed biped. They were enormous: up to 13 inches in length and 6 inches in diameter, and he followed them for some distance, concluding that they belonged to a very accomplished climber. His three Sherpas were so convinced that it was a yeti, they refused to follow him, saying that to even set eyes on a yeti would mean to drop dead instantly. Smythe didn't believe a word of it. He photographed the footprints and later had them analysed by the Natural History Museum in London, who concluded that they were the tracks of a bear. The size of the print was accounted for by snowmelt around the outside, making it appear larger than it was, plus the fact that bears are known to put their hind paws close to their front ones.

More famously, Eric Shipton took a photograph of a yeti's footprint during his 1951 Everest reconnaissance expedition. His Sherpa Sen Tensing was convinced that it belonged to a yeti because both he and Shipton were familiar with the tracks of a bear, and Sen Tensing said he had actually seen a yeti the previous year. Unlike Frank Smythe's Sherpas, he wasn't afraid.

'Yeti will be very frightened tonight, Sahib,' he told Shipton.

'Why?' Shipton replied.

'No one has ever been here before. We will certainly have scared them.'[10]

As recently as the 1980s, the writer Bruce Chatwin interviewed a monk whose aunt had seen a yeti and described it as 'bigger than a man ... with terrible yellow eyes, arms almost touching the ground, red hair growing upwards from the waist, and a white crest on top.'[11]

Chatwin met a Sherpani, Lakpa Doma, who was tending her yaks in the village of Machermo in the Gokyo Valley in 1974 when a yeti 'sprung on her from behind a rock, dragged her to the stream, but then dumped her and went on to slaughter three of the yaks simply by twisting their horns. The beast had the same yellow eyes, big brow-ridges and hollow temples.'

SHERPA HOSPITALITY AS A CURE FOR FROSTBITE

The hard-drinking Lancastrian climber Don Whillans also claimed to have seen a yeti near Machapuchare Base Camp during Chris Bonington's 1970 expedition to the south face of Annapurna. But aside from him and Messner, few westerners have ever seen one, and for many of us their very existence seems ludicrous. Of course, Frank Smythe's Sherpas would easily be able to account for this – if you do see one you're unlikely to live to tell the tale. Which brings me to the point of this post. Whether or not you believe in yetis is largely irrelevant. The question is, would you know what to do if you saw one? If they rattle along on two feet and are such good climbers, how would you be able to escape?

I put this question to my guide when I was trekking in Bhutan, another Himalayan nation where yetis are known to exist. To my surprise, he had some very specific advice.

'If you meet the male yeti, you have to climb up, because they have a big head overlapping the eyes. They can't see you; that's why you have to climb the mountain. But if you see the female yeti, you have to go down because the female yeti has long breasts. It's very hard for her to walk. So you have to use your logic.'

So there we have it. If you see a yeti, don't panic. Simply look at the size of its forehead, confirm your observation by checking out its breasts, then make your escape in the appropriate direction.

5
IS IT OK FOR MOUNTAINEERS TO MISS A PUJA?

6 February 2013

This may be an obscure subject if ever there was one, but one of the perks of writing a mountaineering blog is that every so often I get asked obscure and intriguing questions by email out of the blue. For example, the other day I received this:

> *Have you encountered any situations where client climbers are Islamic, Mormon, Christian or Jewish (monotheistic) and will not participate in the puja ceremony? If so what sort of issues does this cause, if any?*

Those of you who have been following this blog for a while might be forgiven for thinking that I'm not a very religious person, and probably not someone best qualified to comment on spiritual affairs. I don't know why on earth you might think this, but just because I tend to indulge in irreverent banter from time to time doesn't necessarily mean I can't address more earnest matters. So I had a think, picked up my more serious keyboard, and typed out a response that

I hoped would address the question without making me sound too much like Richard Dawkins.

The puja ceremony is an essential part of any mountaineering expedition in the Himalayas using Sherpa support. Sherpas follow a branch of Buddhism that incorporates much of the animist Bon religion that was prevalent in Tibet before Padmasambhava introduced Buddhism there in the eighth century. They believe the summits are the abode of mountain gods who must be appeased before setting foot on the mountain. Prior to the ceremony, at a prominent location in base camp, they build a rock platform containing a small furnace for burning juniper branches and incense. During the ceremony a *lama* (monk) chants mantras and makes offerings to ask the mountain gods for safe passage during the climb. Mountaineers bring all their technical equipment, such as ice axe, boots and crampons, and put them beside the platform to be blessed during the ceremony. Towards the end, a flagpole is erected on the puja platform and prayer flags are draped from it to all corners of base camp, like spokes of a wheel. Rice is thrown into the air three times (an auspicious number) to the cry of *lhagyelo*, which means 'victory to the gods'. Far from 'conquering' the mountain – a term western mountaineers are increasingly leaving behind – we are allowed to climb it only with the permission of the mountain gods.

I've taken part in many puja ceremonies, some without monks (when our Sherpas have had to argue among themselves who should play lama), some with laid-back monks who have joined in with the naturally playful antics of the Sherpas, and some with austere monks who have taken the ceremony very seriously. I even attended one where the kitchen boy was a trainee lama, so he did the chanting for us. What has been common to all of them is a calming atmosphere across base camp.

IS IT OK FOR MOUNTAINEERS TO MISS A PUJA?

I've never encountered anyone refusing to take part in a puja, and I can't imagine this happens often; if the ceremony doesn't take place then the Sherpas won't climb. Most of us don't believe in mountain gods, but whatever our spiritual beliefs, we all know that a happy Sherpa team increases our chances of summit success. That said, the Sherpas are a tolerant people and it's possible they wouldn't mind if someone declined to join in. For example, anyone who's ever taken part in a puja will know that Sherpas love alcohol, and it seems to form an important part of every ceremony. While I've never encountered a climber refusing to take part in the ceremony, I've seen many instances of climbers refusing to drink alcohol, and the Sherpas are not offended by this.

I don't know what would happen if someone refused to take part altogether. Would the Sherpas refuse to climb with them? More likely they would get stick from their teammates for upsetting the Sherpas, for successful expeditions require teamwork and a strong bond of trust between climbers and Sherpas. Ethically, I suppose that if a person can't bring themselves to take part in a ceremony to accommodate the spiritual beliefs of the Sherpas then they should consider climbing without them, but that's just my view and a more religious person may disagree.

There's another reason why mountaineers of all religions should embrace the puja. While we may not believe in mountain gods, most of us are experienced enough to realise that summit success is dependent on forces beyond our control. Whatever our spiritual beliefs, the puja is an opportunity to reflect on this – whether that's praying to whatever god we believe in, keeping our fingers crossed for good luck, or focusing on what needs to be done and telling ourselves not to do anything silly.

SHERPA HOSPITALITY AS A CURE FOR FROSTBITE

*Serap Jangbu Sherpa conducts a puja at
Gasherbrum base camp in Pakistan.*

6
NAWANG GOMBU: HEART OF A TIGER – A REVIEW

16 November 2016

When I watched the 46-minute documentary *Nawang Gombu: Heart of a Tiger* on YouTube last weekend, it had only been watched 151 times before me. This is ridiculous, given that another one of a man opening a beer bottle with a chainsaw had been watched 3,234,053 times (one more than that after you just googled it).

I've mentioned Nawang Gombu previously. He was the nephew of Tenzing Norgay, and one of my chosen ten great Sherpa mountaineers. *Nawang Gombu: Heart of a Tiger* has flaws as far as documentaries go, but it deserves to be watched more widely because of its subject matter.

There is a treasure trove of historical archive footage, and an astonishing number of people have been interviewed to celebrate the life of this extraordinary man: the great and the good of American and Indian Himalayan mountaineering of the 1960s, 1970s and 1980s, almost his entire extended family, as well as friends from his childhood. At times it causes the film to feel disjointed and repetitive as we are rushed through soundbite after soundbite of people making the same point in different words. But you get the overall message: Nawang Gombu was loved and respected by everyone who knew him. And the positive side of this approach is a wealth of endearing anecdotes that help to paint a picture of his character.

The film has a bizarrely shouty narrator who seems to be auditioning for a female version of Brian Blessed (and she is remarkably successful in this respect). It also begins in irritating fashion. The first 60 seconds consist of soundbites trying to answer the perennial question of why people climb.

'Why would we do anything? Why do you ski?' we hear one voice say, clearly irritated by the question.

I might add: why watch celebrity cake-baking contests, or TV talent shows involving rank amateurs? In the case of mountaineering this question has been asked enough times, and enough decent answers have been provided. We don't need to keep asking it.

In Gombu's case this question is answered in more detail later, but without reference to this opening sequence, so we forget that it was asked. His reason is an important one. He was a Sherpa, and although he loved his job, he climbed primarily as a means of supporting his family through school and giving them a route to a better life. This is the same reason climbing Sherpas still do the same job today. As Tenzing Norgay's nephew, Gombu provides a direct link back to the mountaineering pioneers, and his educated offspring interviewed in the film provide evidence that it can be a successful route.

The question passes and Gombu's friends and family tell us about his early life. He was raised near Thame, in the Khumbu region of Nepal, but as a boy he was sent to the Rongbuk Monastery in Tibet to train as a monk. He hated it there. Boys were beaten with sticks if they forgot their prayers, and after a year he escaped and fled back over the

Nangpa La into Nepal. There follows one of those annoying sequences in which about 20 different people (OK, more like five) explain what an amazing achievement it was for an 11-year-old boy to flee over this glaciated pass. Perhaps for western boys, but the Nangpa La is a principal trading route for Nepalis and Tibetans. I've been up it myself. It's true, there are crevasses; but, on the Tibetan side at least, it isn't especially difficult.

Gombu moved to Darjeeling, where his uncle Tenzing took him under his wing. We learn that Gombu was incredibly strong, and although he was only a little over five feet tall, his chest was as broad as a barrel.

We learn about the incident when a 17-year-old Gombu berated expedition leader John Hunt for carrying only one oxygen cylinder during the 1953 British Everest expedition. We are told that this character trait remained with him throughout his life; Gombu liked to speak his mind, and he was not especially diplomatic – 'he called a spade a spade' is how one of his daughters described him – but people regarded this as a good characteristic.

Gombu became an instructor at the Himalayan Mountaineering Institute (HMI) in Darjeeling, an organisation set up by the Indian prime minister Nehru after Tenzing's ascent of Everest in 1953, with Tenzing as its director. The HMI brought Gombu into contact with many American and Indian expedition organisers. He climbed with the Americans Willi Unsoeld and Will Siri on Makalu in 1954, and in 1960 he reached 8,600m on Everest with an Indian expedition.

In 1963, Gombu joined the American attempt on Everest, an expedition that was to turn him and many American climbers into mountaineering superstars. Historically this expedition has become best remembered for Unsoeld and Tom Hornbein's first ascent of the west ridge, in which they traversed the summit and descended its south-east ridge.

At the time, however, it was Gombu's ascent of the south-east ridge with Jim Whittaker that held the spotlight. At 6'5", Whittaker was a foot taller than Gombu, and they made an odd pairing, but together they became the first American and second Sherpa to reach the summit. Whittaker is interviewed at length in the film, and describes their gentlemanly 'you go first', 'no, you go first' sequence as they approached the summit. Eventually they stepped onto it together, avoiding the childish controversy that followed Tenzing and Hillary's ascent.

After the expedition, Gombu and four of his teammates were taken to America. They met President Kennedy, and Whittaker relates a story of how they asked the president to feel Gombu's thigh. The Sherpas were given a giant Cadillac to drive across America. When the police stopped them for speeding, they were let off after complaining 'but officer, don't you know who we are?'

Gombu returned to Darjeeling in high demand. In 1965 he was invited to join another Indian expedition to Everest. He asked them this question:

But I already climbed Everest in 1963. Why should I go there again and again?

He was offered scholarships for two of his children and a plot of land. He was also promised a place in the first summit party. These offers were enough for him to accept. In May that year he reached the summit again, a historic achievement that one of my favourite interviewees in the film, Colonel Narender 'Bull' Kumar (whose nickname is self-evident) describes with a huge grin: 'I used to very proudly introduce him as the only man in the world who has climbed Everest twice.'

Much of the second half of the film focuses on Gombu's later career as a mountain guide in the United States (where he also became the first Sherpa to climb Denali, the highest mountain in North America).

Phil Ershler, one of the founders of American superoperator International Mountain Guides (IMG), relates a story of when he was a novice mountain guide on Mount Rainier. He was nervously glancing around a crowded mountain hut, 'looking like a lost puppy dog', trying to find a spare bunk when Gombu – now a mountaineering legend – slung his own mat and sleeping bag onto a pile of ropes and said 'Phil, you sleep here'. Ershler has a look of awe in his eyes as he delivers the last line of the story: 'And that's how I met Nawang Gombu.'

Much of the final part is given to Gombu's sons and daughters to reminisce about their father. They talk about how tourists used to turn up at their house in Darjeeling as though it were a shrine. When they were still children he used to ask them to write letters for him in English promoting a particular cause or reference for someone he had agreed to help. He became very active in the Sherpa Buddhist Association, an organisation originally set up as the Sherpa Climbers' Association to help the families of Sherpas injured or killed in climbing accidents.

There is a somewhat teary ending to the film. Gombu died as recently as 2011 and he is still fondly remembered. One of his daughters, Rita Gombu Marwah, became a mountaineer herself, and got to within 183m of the summit of Everest in 1984 before turning around when she saw a storm approaching. There is one sequence in which she is translating on behalf of her mother, and both are crying as she completes the sentence.

He was really hard-working and very caring and he always

> *wanted to help people ... he was always concerned about everybody, not only his family but the rest of the people in the community.*

His character is perhaps best summed up by Jim Wickwire, the first American to climb K2, who climbed with Gombu on an expedition to the north face of Everest in 1982. On that occasion, Gombu promised his family he would not try and reach the summit, even though he was still in his forties and easily strong enough. Wickwire said:

> *He was just a great guy to be with in the mountains, never down. He was always optimistic, always up, and that's the kind of person you want to be around on an expedition.*

It's easy to overlook the film's many little faults and annoyances when you consider it as a whole. All the archive footage and interviews make it an excellent historical record, but most of all, it's a great tribute to a man who deserves to be remembered.

7
FOLLOWING THE EVERESTERS

24 April 2013

This time last year, I was lying in a tent at 6,400m at advanced base camp on the north side of Everest, listening to a deafening wind pound against the nylon beside my head. I had very little appetite and an intermittent headache, and when the sun dropped behind the north-east ridge of Changtse, which towered above camp, the temperature was positively Arctic. Those of you who have fallen asleep drunk leaning against a speaker at a party, and woken up lying outside, naked, on a cold patio, will only have some idea of what it felt like. I spent several days there. It was one of the harshest places I've ever been, but as I became better acclimatised I gradually found it more comfortable. The last night I spent there was on my way down from the summit. I was utterly exhausted, but I had just completed an unbelievable experience, and a great sense of achievement was beginning to mingle with a profound joy and relief at being alive. When I set off the following morning, on the last stretch back to base camp over the rough terrain of the East Rongbuk Glacier, I was glad to be leaving – but one year on I miss the place a great deal, and have many happy memories of it.

Every April and May, a few hundred people seek their own version of this experience by trying to climb Everest. Not so long ago we would find out little about these expeditions until months later, when a handful of participants would publish books or journal articles. Now, thanks to the miracle of modern communications, it's possible to watch from the sidelines – which is precisely what I've been doing over the last two or three weeks. Most commercial expedition operators publish expedition dispatches on their websites, and many individual climbers regularly update blogs from base camp. There are also several websites that track all the goings-on and curate and edit content from blogs and dispatches.

The most popular website for expedition news is probably ExplorersWeb,[12] which, as its name implies, publishes all sorts of adventure news: polar exploration, sailing and aviation as well as mountaineering expeditions. It tends to favour news about elite and sponsored climbers or record attempts, but you can find links to posts by lesser climbers from time to time as well. The site has been around for a long time; although it has its critics, it also has a loyal audience of regular readers. Traffic to my own blog increased significantly when my posts were featured on their home page last year.

A refreshing contrast to the sponsor-friendly ExplorersWeb is Alan Arnette's Everest blog.[13] A former commercial client who is a veteran of four Everest expeditions and reached the summit in 2011, Alan is a champion for the quiet majority of lesser climbers: those with full-time jobs and a love of the mountains, but who were further back in the queue when Santa's elves doled out the climbing talent. These are the people who save up for years and train hard to realise their dream of climbing

Everest. Often there is an interesting story behind their motivation – Alan himself lost his mother to Alzheimer's and is now an ambassador for those whose lives have been touched by the disease. While he includes the better-known elite climbers in his Everest coverage, his real passion is the human stories of the lesser climbers, some of whom he profiles in a series of interviews on his blog in the run-up to the Everest season. He publishes a daily summary of events on the mountain with excerpts from climbers' blogs and team dispatches. His Blog of the Day is regarded as the Piolet d'Or of Everest blogging, and my teammate Grant 'Axe' Rawlinson won it a few times last year, much to my envy (I have since made a full recovery and even exchange emails with Axe from time to time). Alan draws on his substantial experience of climbing Everest as a commercial client by describing the sorts of things first-time Everesters are likely to be feeling and experiencing from day to day, such as a trip through the ladders of the Khumbu Icefall or the fun of a puja.

This year the Everest season began with the tragic death of one of the icefall doctors, Mingma Sherpa. The icefall doctors are the Sherpas responsible for finding and maintaining the route through the Khumbu Icefall by fixing ropes and setting up aluminium ladders across crevasses. The icefall is constantly on the move: crevasses open up and giant towers of ice collapse regularly. Maintaining the route is an extremely dangerous full-time job. Hundreds of climbers every year owe their success to the hard work and bravery of the icefall doctors, but these Sherpas are often forgotten about and don't enjoy the prestige of those who accompany climbers to the summit.

News has been more positive since Mingma's accident. There is believed to be more snow on the mountain this year, which should make the routes safer and easier on both the north and south sides. By contrast there was much more rockfall last year, and many sections of blue ice, which are harder to climb. I was surprised to find the north-east ridge more of a rock scramble than the snow plod you expect to find on big Himalayan peaks, and this made summit day mentally exhausting. Early in the season it was extremely windy – this, combined with the increased risk of avalanche and stonefall, means that ropes were fixed much later in the season. This also caused delays to the establishing and stocking of higher camps by Sherpa teams. This year, rope fixing and load carrying is already more advanced and teams on both sides are now on their first rotations up the mountain. On the south side this means climbing through the icefall and into the Western Cwm to begin the process of acclimatising in the higher camps, and on the north side it means trekking up the East Rongbuk Glacier to advanced base camp and having a stab at climbing the North Col Wall.

I have several friends on Everest this year. On the south side I was disappointed to hear that my teammate from last year, Mila Mikhanovskaia, who was hoping to make an ascent without oxygen, departed early after reaching base camp and realising her heart wasn't in it. By contrast another of my erstwhile teammates, 63-year-old Margaret Watroba, known affectionately as Supergran, is still there on the north side climbing with Altitude Junkies. Margaret is something of a local celebrity in Perth, Australia, where she lives, and is now on her fourth successive Everest expedition. She climbed from the south side in 2010 and 2011, and reached the summit on her second attempt. On the north side last year she was ill on summit day and turned around at the Third Step – the only one of us not to reach the summit – and, in a move the Olympic rower Sir Steve Redgrave would be proud of, she returned to base camp and announced in a live radio interview that she would be retiring from mountaineering. Unlike Sir Steve she didn't ask anyone who saw her putting on a crampon to shoot her, but her retirement proved equally premature, and she is back again this year, more determined than ever to join the small band of people who have climbed Everest from both sides.

I have been following the Altitude Junkies team closely. Having been on three 8,000m peak expeditions with them I know many of the Sherpas, and expedition leader Phil Crampton is a good friend. Phil's expedition dispatches are worth reading. Short, pithy and to the point, they are peppered with his dry humour and dubious jokes. He includes anecdotes about members of the team; this gives the dispatches a human touch and enables you to get to know them better.[14] My father likes it when I climb with the Junkies because he can find out what I'm up to from Phil's dispatches. A few years ago, when I climbed Cho Oyu with Jagged Globe (who have a team on the south side of Everest this year), he complained that the only team members mentioned in dispatches were the celebrities, and when the team divided into two summit parties he didn't know which one I was in.

Also in the Junkies team is another old teammate of mine: Robert Kay.[15] I climbed Manaslu with Robert a couple of years ago and we share the same minimalist haircut. Robert was one of the commercial clients interviewed by Alan Arnette in his introduction to the 2013 season. He's a wise old Himalayan head who talks a lot of good sense but is not afraid to admit to mistakes (the bald heads are often the wisest, I find). On Manaslu he took his skis to the summit hoping to ski back down, but found it extremely hard and concluded that reaching the summit of an 8,000er is hard enough without any gimmicks. He also used Viagra on his first Everest attempt, but admitted that it didn't help him to get up (the mountain, that is).

SHERPA HOSPITALITY AS A CURE FOR FROSTBITE

I should also give a shout out to Edita Nichols, who was catapulted around inside a tent when an avalanche struck her camp on Manaslu last year, but dusted herself off and went on to summit. She is aiming to be the first Lithuanian woman to climb Everest, and chose a novel way of preparing for her climb by reading my account of last year's expedition, *The Chomolungma Diaries*, on her Kindle during the flight out to Nepal (yes, I know, I had to mention it didn't I).[16] There is even a US memory champion, Nelson Dellis, on this year's Junkies team. It's unlikely that his abilities will be improved by the long periods at extreme altitude – or indeed the large quantities of red wine and *rakshi* he is certain to have drunk at the Junkies' puja – but at least he didn't forget to pack anything important.

News will be quieter for the next few days while teams are in the higher camps where communications are patchy, but there are sure to be some stirring stories emerging over the next month. Numbers on the mountain are reported as being similar to last year, when there were 800 climbers with summit permits on the south side (of which 335 were paying westerners and the rest Sherpas) and around 200 on the north side (with roughly a 50/50 split between Sherpas and westerners). This year there have been 315 summit permits issued on the south and around 100 on the north. Last year the weather was poor and there were only four days with suitable summit conditions, leading to congestion. Ten people died, but there were around 500 successful summits and 300 new summiteers.

We are all hoping that the mountain gods grant a longer summit window this year, which means the summit attempts can be spread out and conditions should be safer.

Our team of commercial clients and Sherpas underneath the prayer flags at Everest base camp in Tibet, 2012.

PART TWO

CONFLICT

8
ALL YOU NEED TO KNOW ABOUT THE EVEREST FIST FIGHT

29 April 2013

For those who have been asking for an insightful analysis of the punch-up on the Lhotse Face over the weekend, I'm not going to disappoint you. But first, some background for those of you who may have missed it.

Superstar climbers Ueli Steck and Simone Moro, and their cameraman Jon Griffith, were involved in an altercation with a team of Sherpas who were fixing ropes at 7,400m near Camp 3 on Everest. When they returned to Camp 2, the climbers were confronted by an angry mob of Sherpas, and allegedly had to flee for their lives through the Khumbu Icefall back to base camp. Those are the bare bones, but much more has been published elsewhere.[17]

In fact, as usual people have been falling over themselves to report the story without waiting for the facts to emerge, and it's been hard to tell truth from fiction.

'The reasons behind the attack are complicated and deep-rooted and to do with the relationship between westerners and Nepalis on the mountain over many years,' commented Jon Griffith on Facebook, according to a report on the BMC website.[18] The incident was due to a clash of civilisations and two types of climbing style – commercial expeditions and purist – the *Nepali Times* reported.[19] It was an uprising against the way Nepalis feel treated by westerners, the three climbers said in a joint statement, according to the *Daily Mail*, who also reported that the climbers are continuing with their expedition.[20]

'Total bollocks, we are leaving Nepal as soon as we can,' Jon Griffith apparently told the Telegraph.[21]

The Sherpas reacted aggressively because the climbers were moving unroped and much faster, and this caused their pride to be wounded, the BBC reported the climbers as saying (presumably swapping their ice axes for a spade to dig a bigger hole for themselves).[22] More amusingly the Nepali newswire that originally broke the story reported the climbers names as Simboli Moro and Wool Stick, and many mainstream media outlets such as the *Daily Mail* and the *Daily Express* simply copied and pasted the story without bothering to do any basic fact checking. This had a surprisingly positive effect on their readers, who were so bemused by Wool Stick's name that only two of them remembered to make racist remarks in the comments section.[23]

But is any of this true, or is it all just idle speculation? Well, the *Footsteps on the Mountain* team is not averse to joining the stampede for a quick story, so here is the insightful analysis I promised.

The insightful analysis

I can confirm that the following three factors were involved in the altercation:

- Wounded pride

ALL YOU NEED TO KNOW ABOUT THE EVEREST FIST FIGHT

- Provocation
- Too much testosterone

And there we have it. The brawl happened because of wounded pride, provocation and too much testosterone. In fact, the only standard ingredient missing was alcohol. I can also reveal that the consequences of the fight were:

- A westerner's perspective (freely available on many blogs and websites)
- A Sherpa perspective (completely unavailable, even if you happen to know a climbing Sherpa you can ask)

And one other thing:

- Simboli Moro and Wool Stick are joke names, like Sillius Soddus and Biggus Dickus

The final word was left for climbing legend Stephen Venables, first Briton to climb Everest without supplementary oxygen, who tweeted a photo of two climbers in hard hats waving V-signs against a mountain backdrop. He didn't say whether it was his own photo and if these were friends of his, but he'd Photoshopped on a speech bubble.[24]

'You touch my ropes and I'll knock your xxxxxxx head off!!!!' it said.

And there we have it. If you think this post has been unnecessarily frivolous, even by the standards of this blog, don't worry – normal service will be resumed on Wednesday.

9
A TRIBUTE TO SHERPAS, THE TIGERS OF THE SNOW

15 *May 2013*

May 1934, Bareilly Railway Station, India. Two suited Englishman and a Sherpa are running up and down a platform, screaming at the top of their voices and peering into the carriages of a crowded train, trying to locate two companions they have arranged to meet. Their luggage is packed away inside another train to Kathgodam, due to depart in ten minutes; their companions are Sherpas who have never travelled on a train in their lives and don't speak a word of Hindi. Indian railway stations are chaotic places at the best of times. Unless the Englishmen can find the Sherpas and help them, it seems unlikely they will be able to find the connecting train on their own.

But despite their eccentric performance the train pulls away, much to the relief of the passengers squeezed inside, and there is still no sign of the two Sherpas. A whistle sounds. The Englishmen realise that their connecting train is about to depart too. They sprint to another platform and run alongside the train, trying to locate the carriage with their luggage. Suddenly the smaller of the two Englishmen tugs the shirt sleeve of the other one and points inside one of the carriages. Sitting inside it, comfortably ensconced among the luggage and eating oranges without a care in the world, are the two Sherpas.

The two Englishmen are the great mountain explorers Eric Shipton and Bill Tilman, and this will not be the first time they come to appreciate the resourcefulness of their Sherpa companions. Over the following five months Shipton, Tilman, Angtharkay, Pasang and Kusang make a thorough exploration of the Garhwal region of India. They become the first people to find a way into the Nanda Devi Sanctuary, a secret haven surrounded by high mountains; they cross two watersheds through thick jungle in the rainy monsoon season, at times surviving on a diet of tree mushrooms and bamboo shoots; and they return to the Sanctuary to look for a plausible route up Nanda Devi, the highest mountain in the region, believed to be the abode of a goddess. They hire local porters for some of the journey, but often find them unreliable. By contrast the three Sherpas never falter, carrying huge loads over dangerously precipitous terrain. They pitch camp, cook, and help to organise the porter loads. Despite the harsh living conditions, they continue tirelessly without complaint. In fact, Shipton and Tilman find them to be the best possible companions, unfailingly cheerful and possessed of a great sense of humour, always ready to share a joke and laugh at the situations they find themselves in.

Sherpa mob violence?

This is the nostalgic picture of Sherpas that many people share – of a race of genial and hard-working mountain men. It may seem romantic, but it's a picture that many travellers to Nepal, who have spent weeks in the mountains trekking and climbing with Sherpas, take home with them.

But last month that picture changed when three western mountaineers, Ueli Steck from Switzerland, the Italian Simone Moro, and Jon Griffith from the United Kingdom, abandoned their expedition to Everest, returning home with a bizarre story of mob violence at 6,400m in the Western Cwm. They were ambushed at Camp 2 by a group of 100 masked Sherpas, armed with stones and knives, who threatened to kill them. The reports said that Simone Moro was dragged from his tent on his knees, and made to beg forgiveness – and that he would have been summarily executed with a rock had another western climber not intervened and saved him. They fled back to base camp in terror and were so scared they had to find an alternative route through the Khumbu Icefall, away from the fixed ropes and ladders put in place for other climbers.

For days on end their story was reported in the western media.[25] Journalists and their readers speculated on its cause. How could a people known for their cheerfulness, hard work and humility have become so violent? The dispute had nothing to do with their own actions, the climbers were reported as saying, but were a result of tensions between westerners and Sherpas that had been building up over 20 years. Everest has become too overcrowded, the media reported, and is now a powder keg. An incident like this was inevitable; the Sherpas are fed up with being mistreated by westerners and were due to rebel. Others claimed that Sherpas have a tribal streak and club together in stressful situations.

But hidden behind the sensationalism were alternative versions of the story that went largely unreported. One of the few Sherpas who spoke out was Lhakpa, owner of the Nepali mountaineering operator Himalayan Ascent. He said there were many Sherpas and westerners in the Western

Cwm that day and not all of them were part of the conflict. Most tried to intervene and calm the situation, but tensions were running high; violence broke out when a westerner tussled with a Sherpa. According to his account the incident had more in common with a pub brawl than a lynch mob.[26]

With such wildly conflicting stories it's hard for an objective observer to guess what actually happened. What most people seem to agree is that the incident was ignited when the three westerners at the centre of it climbed up the Lhotse Face alongside the Sherpa rope-fixing team, who were responsible for preparing the route for commercial teams. Because the job of rope fixing is tough and dangerous, there is an unwritten rule that westerners should not climb the face until it is complete. But because they were climbing unsupported and did not need to use the fixed ropes, the three westerners considered themselves exempt from the rule. When they crossed the place where the Sherpas were fixing the route in order to reach their camp, the Sherpas objected. Their leader and Simone Moro exchanged angry words. Bizarrely, later evidence suggests that Moro may have used the word 'motherfucker' in Nepali while one of the Sherpas was broadcasting to Camp 2 on his radio, and this caused unrest among some of the younger Sherpas listening in.

What's certain is that an incident occurred in the Western Cwm that should not have happened, an unidentified number of Sherpas used unacceptable levels of violence, and it must have been a frightening experience for the climbers involved. When more eyewitnesses finish their expeditions and return home we will hear more about it, but until then the accounts of the three climbers at the centre of it hold sway. While the real story is likely to be somewhere between the two extremes, it is their version that has generally been taken to be accurate by the media and readers, and the tendency to sensationalise, provoke hate, make judgements and generalise means the reputation of Sherpas in the west has been damaged unfairly.

The violence that took place should be addressed by the Nepali authorities, the Sherpa community, and the teams whose members were involved, but it should not reflect on Sherpas as a whole. Many people who have never been to Nepal, met a Sherpa, or have any historical perspective on their relations with western climbers have been quick to give their opinion of Sherpas as a race and explain why the altercation happened.

Those who think the incident on Everest this year springs from tensions between Sherpas and westerners over the last 20 years should learn, for example, about the 1953 Everest expedition, when the British had Tenzing to thank for quelling a mutiny right at the start of the expedition. On his return to Kathmandu after reaching the summit Tenzing was swept along by a crowd of eager Nepalis waving flags and banners, and crying, *'Tenzing zindabad!'* ['Long live Tenzing!']. Nepalis and Indians alike claimed him as their own, and asked him to sign statements saying that he reached the summit before Hillary. The nationalist fervour led to tensions between Tenzing and his British teammates. There were angry statements in the press from both sides. You can look for the roots of a conflict anywhere if you want to, but sometimes the explanation is simpler.

A personal perspective on Sherpas

This is a post I have been meaning to write for a while, and the incident on Everest last month has given urgency to it. Much has been written by westerners about Sherpas over the last century – but the voice of the Sherpas themselves is rare indeed. I can't provide it either, but I can provide my own perspective of a people who have given me many happy memories, taken me to places I could never have been without them, and put their lives at risk to help me. I don't recall a single violent incident. It saddens me to read some of the things that have been written about them over the last few weeks. If I can do anything to help restore their reputation, I will, and if this account also seems romantic, it is with good reason.

Not all Sherpas are elite mountaineers, but there are a remarkable number who are. Many disparaging comments have been written about Sherpa climbing skills over the last few weeks – that they lack the technical ability of the top western climbers. This may be true, but it misses the point. Technical climbing ability is rarely the most important quality in Himalayan mountaineering. The capacity to endure hardship, perform with immense strength at extreme altitudes, and ferry heavy loads over steep terrain are much more important skills to have on most routes. Here the Sherpas are among the elite; sure, there are western climbers who are just as strong, but they are the exception rather than the norm, and are usually at the top of the pecking order. Sherpas are often the workhorses, carrying out their work without complaint and with great dignity, yet they are the Premiership footballers of high-altitude mountaineering. They take the greatest risk in preparing the route for western climbers. The icefall doctors are under constant risk of avalanche and ice collapse. Of the four climbers who have died on Everest so far this year, three have been Sherpas. NSPCC ambassador David Tait was reported to be one of the first to summit on 10 May this year, yet he was following right behind the Sherpa rope-fixing team, who arrived first and made the route safe for him and all the other climbers who will summit from the south this year.

I have trekked, climbed and travelled with Sherpas ever

since my first visit to Nepal in 2002. Many earn a living as mountain guides, cooks and porters on western treks and expeditions. Most of them like a drink, and I have bought them many. They are always willing to share a joke and see the funny side of life. I am forever in awe of their strength and stamina at high altitude, and their courage over dangerous terrain.

My first encounter with elite climbing Sherpas was in 2007, on 7,546m Muztag Ata in western China. Three Sherpas were with us there. All of them had summited Everest that year. There were a couple of occasions when I arrived in a high camp and began to carve out a platform for my tent. It was unbelievably hard work after an exhausting climb at high altitude, and I never got very far before a Sherpa arrived and took over. I rested and let them get on with it; without their help my climb would have been so much more exhausting. The day after our successful summit, they were packing away our high camp at 6,800m and I asked if there was anything I could help them to carry. One of the Sherpas, Gyalzen, looked around for a few seconds before selecting two foam mattresses, which looked very bulky by the time I had tied them to the outside of my pack, but weighed next to nothing. This was typical behaviour for a Sherpa: happy to shoulder most of the burden, while allowing his clients to feel good about themselves.

In 2009 I completed a happy trek in the Khumbu with my friend Mark Dickson and a crew of 13 Nepalis, most of whom were Sherpas. We climbed two popular trekking peaks, Mera Peak and Island Peak, and crossed a difficult technical pass, the Amphu Labtse, which involved scaling ice walls and abseiling down rock overhangs. We completed the crossing with technical equipment, including crampons, ices axes, carabiners and climbing harnesses, but our Sherpa porters had none of that, happily completing the crossing with heavy loads carried on their foreheads using head straps. I watched nervously from a ledge on the far side as the loads were lowered on ropes down a short vertical section. The Sherpas happily skipped down after, using only an arm wrap on a fixed rope for security. I abseiled down behind them, but got into a spot of bother when I reached the bottom of the rope at an anchor point and found myself turning upside down. I righted myself and started climbing back up the rock as far as I could, but before I could solve the problem on my own, one of the porters waiting at the bottom, Drukchen, noticed my predicament, ran up the ice slope I intended to abseil down, tossed me a rope, and legged it back down again. When I finally reached the bottom an older porter, Lhakpa, was there to take my arm and guide me to a wider ledge. I didn't need the help of either man – in many ways it was embarrassing – but they both considered it their duty to offer assistance to a westerner who found the terrain harder than they did.

In 2009 on Gasherbrum II, an 8,000m peak in Pakistan, we were the only team on the mountain with Sherpa support. One evening we were lying in our tents at Camp 1 in the Gasherbrum Cwm when a light began flashing on the mountain over 1,500m above us. A climber had gone missing close to the summit the previous day and was believed to be dead. Now here he was signalling his distress in the darkness high above. There were many climbers at Camp 1 that day, and within minutes they had gathered outside our tents, even though the climber in trouble was not attached to our party. We were the only team with Sherpas. Everyone knew that, were a rescue to be carried out, only Sherpas would be quick and strong enough to reach the man and bring him down safely. It is ever the way on the commercial 8,000m peaks; Sherpas have saved many lives. They are true heroes, but often their help is taken for

SHERPA HOSPITALITY AS A CURE FOR FROSTBITE

granted, as it was that day on Gasherbrum.

When I embarked on my summit push on the north side of Everest last year, I had twice been up the North Col Wall, and once to the North Col itself at 7,060m. But our Sherpas had been all the way to Camp 3 at 8,210m, establishing our camps and leaving vital supplies such as oxygen cylinders ready for us as we arrived at the camps on our summit push. Even so, I found it incredibly tough, and my backpack seemed heavy. I would never have managed had our Sherpas not done all that work for us in preparing the way. My summit day took 18 hours, and my personal Sherpa, Chongba, stayed with me throughout, making sure I got back to Camp 3 safely. Another Sherpa, Ang Gelu, gave me a helping hand on the Second Step when I found myself struggling up smooth rock. I owe them my success – perhaps my life. We had a very happy expedition with a good relationship between Sherpas and westerners. I don't know what they say about us behind our backs, perhaps they laugh about us, but if so then they disguise it well. We shared a celebratory drink with them on several occasions during our return to Kathmandu. Personally, I believe that our friendship was genuine.

When I see some of the things that have been written about Sherpas over the last few weeks by people who have never shared these experiences, it's difficult to know how to react. Should I laugh or should I be angry? Everest is a powder keg, they say. Sherpas are fed up with being mistreated by foreigners over many years and are ready to rebel if they're not given more power. They think that Everest is their mountain, and are jealous of any climbers who appear to be better than them.

These descriptions could be about different people in a different world. They don't match the Sherpas I know.

Even if the statements were accurate, they are almost

childishly trivial. Of course Everest is their mountain. Half of it lies in their country, the Khumbu, and if anyone has earned the right to determine what happens there in the future, it is the Sherpas. The ones who climb Everest are highly respected within their community, and earn an income far in excess of what their ancestors who perished in the avalanche in 1922 could ever have dreamed of. But when I shared a glass of Everest beer with our climbing Sherpas in Sam's Bar, Kathmandu, after our expedition, and asked them whether they hoped their children would follow in their footsteps, they all said no. They wanted to send their children to good schools so they could become educated in a way they hadn't themselves. They all believed that education was the route to prosperity – not high-altitude mountaineering.

Whether you believe Lhakpa Sherpa's account of the Everest fight last month to be the accurate version or not, his was a rare educated Sherpa voice providing a Sherpa perspective, and he made one statement we should all take to heart.

> *As a Nepali-owned outfitter, we often hear our western outfitter friends acknowledge that the skilled Sherpa climbers deserve more. But what are they actually willing to give more of? More money? More benefits? More fame? Perhaps they should start with more respect.*[27]

Another rare Sherpa voice is that of Tashi Sherpa, owner of the outdoor clothing manufacturer Sherpa Adventure Gear. In an interview with Ed Douglas for *The Guardian* shortly after the Everest fight, he addressed the allegation of 20 years of Sherpa frustration by saying he didn't think there was any frustration, and that Sherpas were treated a lot better than they were 10 years ago.[28]

SHERPA HOSPITALITY AS A CURE FOR FROSTBITE

As Sherpas become better educated and more westernised, it is inevitable that they will begin to assert more authority over expeditions to the Himalayas, and rightly so. After all, on Alaska's Denali, the highest mountain in North America, only a handful of American companies are allowed to operate, and foreign operators must all subcontract their services. While this may be taking things too far, I for one will not complain if the Sherpa voice, silent for so long, becomes louder in the coming years.

This has been a long, personal post, and if you have read all the way to the end, thank you sincerely – it means a lot. You probably feel like you have just climbed a huge Himalayan mountain. In true Sherpa style, go and get yourself a beer.

Temba Sherpa, Pasang Lama, Tarke Sherpa and Pasang Gombu Sherpa at Gasherbrum base camp, 2009.

10
EXPEDITION DISPATCH: THE SHERPA SACRIFICE

20 April 2014

I don't know whether this is going to post successfully, as we have been without meaningful internet communications since we arrived at Everest Base Camp over a week ago. I have wandered down to Gorak Shep in search of 3G or Wi-Fi to try and send it from my iPhone. It may not work, but I have to try, because too much has happened to remain silent, and we need to provide our story before the facts are swallowed up by media hyperbole.

On Friday morning we awoke early to make our first short foray into the Khumbu Icefall. We didn't intend to climb far, perhaps for two to three hours before returning to our camp for lunch. At 6.45am I was wandering slowly through the sprawl of base camp, lost in my thoughts, when Jay, walking behind me, gave a cry.

'Hey, Mark, have you seen that? Take a look up there!'

I looked up in time to see a giant cloud on the skyline: one of the biggest avalanches I had ever seen, swallowing up the entire width of the icefall. Up ahead of us Ian, Robert, Kevin and Louis were walking together when they heard a loud crack and looked up to see a huge section of ice collapse off the West Shoulder, triggering the avalanche we saw sweeping across the icefall.

'Man, this is bad news. There's people up there,' Robert said when we arrived at the base of the icefall, where we had intended to put on our crampons.

It wasn't until our sirdar Dorje arrived a few minutes later that we began to realise the scale of the horror that was about to unfold.

'How many Sherpa?' I asked him, pointing up the icefall.

'Maybe forty, fifty,' he replied.

It became immediately obvious that our foray would be off. It would take us many hours to reach the avalanche site, and we were not acclimatised. We would only get in the way of any rescue. The Sherpas are much stronger than we are; they were fully acclimatised and had been carrying loads up the icefall for days to help establish our higher camps. It was Sherpas who were caught up there in the avalanche, and it would be Sherpas who would carry out any rescue (or, as it happened, assist in the recovery of bodies). For the most part we western climbers would be helpless witnesses to the biggest tragedy in Everest history.

Dorje and Ang Gelu headed up the icefall immediately. Our expedition leader Phil Crampton radioed back to camp to try and rouse more of our Sherpa team to help. They had returned from the icefall only the day before and were having a well-earned rest, but four of them, Pasang Ongchu, Kami, Kusang and Samden, put on their climbing gear and arrived only minutes later. Phil headed into the icefall with them, but his main priority was to pull them off the mountain if it became too dangerous up there. He knew they would be carrying out the bulk of the work.

I walked up onto a ridge of ice and stood to watch for the next two hours. Initially things seemed quite hopeful. We could see figures emerging from the ice. Dozens of them appeared near a section on the skyline known as the Football Field, precisely where we saw the snow billowing. Ones and twos appeared lower down, heading downwards. There could easily be 40 or 50 of them and they were all moving, if only slowly. It seemed a miracle!

But there was bad news as well. Radios were crackling all around us, and we heard that four Sherpas from the Discovery Channel expedition were missing. Another Sherpa was critically injured.

At nine o'clock I wandered slowly back to our camp, where I removed my climbing gear, washed myself, and sat down to watch with the rest of our team. Everyone – including our other Sherpas, many of whom had friends and family up there – could do little else but stand outside and watch events unfold.

The tragedy was deepening. Somebody said that 13 Sherpas were now dead or missing – we couldn't be sure. At ten o'clock the first helicopters appeared. One of them landed up on the ice of the Football Field and brought down some casualties. Then hundreds of people watched in horror as body after body was brought down, swinging beneath one of the helicopters on a long line. It was relentless. We lost count of the number of times the chopper returned to the icefall. Every so often we imagined the body moving on landing, and hoped it was a survivor, but mostly they were motionless.

At lunchtime Phil returned with our six tireless Sherpas. Dorje and Ang Gelu supervised while the other four did much of the digging out of bodies. It's hard to imagine what it must have been like up there.

We now believe that 14 Sherpas are confirmed dead and three more are still missing. If all these deaths are confirmed, it will be an unprecedented disaster in the annals of

Himalayan mountaineering, eclipsing Mallory and his Sherpas in 1922 and even the Germans on Nanga Parbat in the 1930s.

As for the Khumbu Icefall, the first person to die there was an American – Jake Breitenbach, in 1963 – when a serac collapsed as he was helping to establish a route through. There have been many fatalities since, but never on this scale. Decades ago westerners shared much of the risk, but it's different now. On Friday we shared neither the loss with our Sherpas nor the risk. We were to make our first short journey into the icefall, but our Sherpas had been through twice already.

Our lack of internet access means we are happily protected from the media storm that I'm sure has accompanied this tragedy. I've seen enough in the past to be able to predict the headlines, though: 'Rich western tourists send Sherpas to their deaths to satisfy their egos and tick off their bucket list by climbing Everest'.

While there is an element of truth in this it's only a fraction of the full story. Journalists who write these headlines haven't been here and looked up into the icefall with their boots on, ready to go up. They don't understand the motivations of mountaineers (both Sherpa and westerner) and the calculated risks we all take to do what we enjoy, and nor do they have an appreciation of the historical background that has led to Sherpas becoming the tigers of Himalayan mountaineering.

After this latest tragedy some teams will remain on the mountain and others will pack up and leave. These decisions will be based on the wishes of the Sherpas, as we all know that we cannot climb the mountain without them. Chomolungma belongs to the Sherpas and it's only right they have an increasing say in what happens here. But the history of Everest has involved Sherpas and westerners working hand in hand, and the future of Everest will be better if this remains the case.

We are lucky in the Altitude Junkies team. We will have a few days of rest now to come to terms with what has happened. We will probably hold another puja to appease the mountain gods, and then we will continue with what we came to do. Our Sherpa dining tent is normally out of bounds, but on Friday night they invited us in to share rum and Tuborg. There was no us and them. We have different roles and of course they work much harder than we do, but we are a team working together.

This is the way Friday's sad events should be treated: not by apportioning blame, but by trying our best to share the loss some of us feel more keenly than others.

Lighting butter lamps for the 16 mountain workers who died in the Khumbu Icefall, 2014.

11
LHOTSE 2014: THE WORLD'S MOST EXPENSIVE EVEREST BASE CAMP TREK

22 *May 2014*

The story of the Altitude Junkies 2014 Everest and Lhotse expedition

I'm pretty experienced at failing to get up 8,000m peaks. It took me four attempts to summit my first one, and I quickly learned that the most important thing is not to reach the summit but to enjoy the whole experience of trying and failing and trying again, because however well prepared you are the weather can always thwart you. I was progressing smoothly with my modest ambition of reaching Camp 2 on all fourteen 8,000ers, an ambition that seemed quite achievable and provided me with some satisfying climbing.

I was excited to be attempting 8,516m Lhotse, the fourth-highest mountain in the world, which stands across the South Col from Everest. I climbed Everest from the north side two years ago and I was keen to sample the south-side experience and visit the places I had read so much about. I wanted to follow in the footsteps of Tenzing and Hillary, wanted to climb through the tumbling seracs of the Khumbu

THE WORLD'S MOST EXPENSIVE EVEREST BASE CAMP TREK

Icefall. If you're a regular reader of my blog you will also know that I'm often upset about the negative media coverage about Everest, which is at odds with my own experience of climbing the mountain from the north. Much of that coverage focuses on the south side of Everest; I wanted to find out for myself how closely it resembles the truth. Lhotse shares a base camp with Everest, and follows the same climbing route through the Khumbu Icefall to the Western Cwm and all the way up to Camp 3 on the Lhotse Face. By attempting Lhotse I would learn about the south-side Everest experience while climbing a new 8,000er. Or so I hoped. Even if I didn't reach the summit, I would surely at least reach Camp 2, as I had on every previous occasion.

I was also excited when I met the rest of my team at the Courtyard Hotel in Kathmandu. Climbing with the mountaineering company Altitude Junkies is a bit like climbing with old college friends: the Junkies have so many repeat clients that on every expedition there will be people I know, and there will be others I know a little about because they know the people I know. This year we had seven clients on Everest and five on Lhotse. Expedition leader Phil Crampton introduced those of us on Lhotse permits – Louis, Edita, Margaret, Ian and myself – as the Dream Team, because we had all climbed Everest and had 27 8,000m peak expeditions between us; but, with me and my drinking buddy Ian Cartwright in the team, it would have to be quite a bad dream. We didn't know then that our dream would become a nightmare.

The expedition started with something of a novelty: a visit to the Ministry of Culture, Tourism and Civil Aviation (MoCTCA) for a briefing aimed at promoting peace and harmony on the mountain. I already had a low opinion of MoCTCA because of a series of bizarre announcements they made to the media in the run-up to the season. This farcical briefing confirmed my belief that Nepal's highest tourist body is being run by people with little understanding of mountain tourism. We all found it funny at the time, but this simple fact was to have serious consequences for everyone later.

That evening we had a team meal at Jatra Restaurant in Thamel. Phil produced a special menu for us with the following line printed at the top: 'Please drink responsibly Ian, Mark, Margaret and Louis, as I'm paying for the alcohol'. Ian proceeded to ignore this request, and Edita was so offended not to be listed that she spent much of the expedition trying to ensure she gets a mention on the menu next time.

Two days later, on 3 April, we flew by helicopters to Lukla to begin our trek to Everest Base Camp. Sending us by private chopper was a good move on Phil's part – it has become the only sensible means of getting there. The scary aircraft landing at Lukla is a remarkable experience, but after a series of accidents it's no longer a reliable means of reaching the Everest region. The Twin Otter planes have not been well maintained by airlines, there are only half as many of them as there once were, and rules for landing have been tightened. Having to wait for days for a flight has now become the norm. Many holidays have been ruined; some insurance companies have even stopped covering the flights. It's bad news for the people of the Khumbu region, who are now keen to extend the road to Lukla instead of relying on aviation. Tourist numbers are down, and I was surprised how quiet it was during our first few days on the trail.

That first night we stayed at the Buddha Lodge in Phakding, owned by the family of our sirdar Dorje Sherpa. Some of the team spent the afternoon watching the 1996 *Everest* IMAX movie on the 40in screen in the dining room there. It's not the way IMAX movies are meant to be watched, but Dorje is famous for being one of the men who carried David Breashears's 17kg IMAX camera to the summit, so the viewing was special for a different reason. I sat upstairs in my room reading and was surprised to hear guffaws of laughter coming from downstairs. I had watched the movie in the IMAX cinema in London Waterloo a few years ago, and I didn't remember it being particularly funny. I later found out that they had watched a couple of episodes of the puerile British comedy *The Inbetweeners* afterwards. Mel, our Chinese team member, spent his afternoon more fruitfully. An architect by trade, we discovered that he's also a brilliant artist when at dinner he produced a most amazing pencil sketch of the teahouses of Phakding and their mountain skyline.

The trail from Phakding to the Sherpa capital of Namche Bazaar passes through the wooded Dudh Kosi gorge, with impressive cliffs on either side. For much of the way the holy mountain of Khumbila rose up as a perfect white pyramid straight ahead. While the scenery is dramatic, this part of the trail isn't particularly remote. We encountered villages and teahouses at almost every turn, and there seemed to be an unaccountable array of police, army and national park checkpoints manned by staff who were determined to take our permits off us for safekeeping (quite what they expected us to do at the next checkpoint without them I can only imagine).

Today the first signs emerged that Dream Team wasn't perhaps the most accurate moniker for us Lhotse climbers. Something Louis ate didn't agree with him, and he arrived at breakfast claiming to have been to the toilet 40 times already that morning. He was badly dehydrated and couldn't walk far without having to stop and fertilise the bushes along the trail. But Everest summiteers who struggle on an easy trek don't get much sympathy. Louis's fiercest critic was his wife Dia, who was joining us for the trek to base camp. When her words of encouragement ('You've climbed Everest – stop being so pathetic!') failed to provide the necessary stimulation, more drastic measures were called for. They next tried to find somewhere they could hire a horse to carry him up to Namche. When this failed Louis was rescued by Robert and his friend Scott, a surgeon who was also coming along for the trek to base camp. Robert pulled out his climbing harness and Prusik cords and proceeded to short-rope Louis up the trail, while Scott produced a needle and injected him with dexamethasone. These are tried-and-trusted mountaineering techniques that have been used many times to get exhausted climbers down from summits, but would they enable Louis to plod up the forested hillside to Namche? In the end he made it under his own steam, much to the disappointment of Phil, who was hoping he would arrive on all fours and had spent the afternoon thinking up horse jokes ('Why are you always making an ass of yourself, Louis?').

Namche is one of the most spectacularly sited villages anywhere, with colourful rooftops climbing above a horseshoe-shaped bowl in a hillside. The Bhote Kosi River crashes by hundreds of metres below and the dramatic snow-capped peak of Kongde Ri rises up on the other side of the valley. We saw nothing of this on our rest day the following day, when a damp grey mist hung over the village, but the next few days took us through indescribably beautiful landscapes – some of the world's most popular for a reason. As we rose above the tree line on trails clinging to hillsides high above dramatic river valleys, the land became increasingly alpine, with dwarf species of juniper and rhododendron giving way to rocky moonscapes. Grandest of all were the mountains, most of them horribly technical climbs up fluted spires of ice; Thamserku, Kangtega and

Ama Dablam dominated the skyline to our right for the next two days, with Everest and Lhotse soaring above the rocky mountain wall of Nuptse at the end of the valley.

We spent a rest day in Dingboche, where the trail turns north into the main Khumbu Valley that leads to the foot of Everest. There we acclimatised by climbing up to a viewpoint 700m above the village. Everest and Lhotse had disappeared behind a smaller peak, Pokalde; but two more 8,000ers, Cho Oyu and Makalu, were visible on separate horizons. More impressive still was a trio of vertical rock towers crowned with snow – Taboche Peak, Cholatse and Arakam Tse – that rose to our left and remained with us for the next two days as we journeyed north. Despite their prominence in a popular mountain area, these peaks have had very few ascents, and it was easy to see why.

A new mountain vista opened before us as we climbed up to the Thokla Pass and the stone memorials to those who have died on Everest. As we walked alongside the lateral moraine of the Khumbu Glacier the base camp peaks appeared before us: triangular Pumori, wedge-shaped Lingtren and the crumpled black wall of Nuptse. I spent my rest day in Lobuche high up on that ridge of moraine savouring the wide mountain panorama and revelling in the tranquillity and silence of nothing but the wind. Although it was my fourth time in the Khumbu region I had never been this far up the valley before. People talk about how busy it is, but you don't need to move very far off the trail to feel like you're miles from anywhere – as indeed you are. Yaks were grazing on the short grass just below me, but everywhere else was snow, rock and sky, supporting no life but those of us who love the mountains.

The following day, 11 April, we completed the final section of the dusty trail and arrived in the natural amphitheatre of Everest Base Camp, surrounded by towering walls of rock. It's a place I've long imagined being in, and at last I was seeing it for the very first time. At first I was confused. Across the Lho La I could see Everest's north peak of Changtse, a peak I knew well from my ascent of the north side, and I recognised many of the others from photos – Pumori, Lingtren, Khumbutse and the West Shoulder – but I could see no sign of the Khumbu Icefall. The reason for this only became clear when I was very close to base camp. The icefall really is a secret opening into the Western Cwm and Everest's upper reaches from the south side. It remained hidden from view until I was much closer. Everest appeared to be completely guarded by impossible faces, and for a long time I gazed at the hanging glaciers and rock wall of the Lho La thinking it must be the Khumbu Icefall. When they first explored Everest from the south side in 1950, Bill Tilman and Charles Houston must have gone right to the top end of the valley before they saw the route up into the Western Cwm and realised it might be climbable. Eventually, as I approached the sprawling tented village of base camp below me on the glacier, the mass of frozen blocks spilling down between the steep walls of the West Shoulder and Nuptse was obvious, and the Khumbu Icefall then became the most dominant feature of the landscape: the dangerous road we all knew we must travel through several times before our adventure would be complete.

We settled into the familiar comfort of the Altitude Junkies base camp. We each had our own two-man tent to sleep in. There were two sizeable bathroom tents with toilet, shower and sink, a storage tent for all our kit, a kitchen tent and a comfortable dining tent with carpet and heaters. We were introduced to our Sherpa team. Half of them I know well from previous expeditions, including Chongba, who was with me on the summits of Manaslu and Everest and with whom I would be climbing again. But the 30-strong

Sherpa team was twice the size it's been on previous expeditions. Luckily for us, the US operator Mountain Trip had been unable to get a team together for Everest this year, but their loss was our gain; we were able to employ their experienced Everest Sherpas ourselves. Later that afternoon I reacquainted myself with one of the most enjoyable aspects of an Altitude Junkies expedition: base camp happy hour, when we gather in the dining tent for red wine, cheese and Pringles.

Two days later, on 13 April, we had our puja ceremony straight after breakfast. A lama had come from Pangboche Monastery to chant prayers beneath our puja platform and ask the mountain gods for safe passage. I don't know what we did differently from other teams; this year the mountain gods were angry, yet they decided to be kind to us. The lama kept the ceremony relatively short, and finished his chanting after about an hour. A flagpole was raised onto the platform and prayer flags strung to all the corners of camp. We threw rice into the air, cries of *lhagyelo* rang out, and we were each presented with a tiny book of prayers to hang round our necks for the remainder of the expedition.

Then the lama departed for his next puja and the drinking started. Not all teams indulge in this particular part of the ceremony as eagerly as the Junkies. It's not without reason we are known as the Drunkies. I blame our Sherpas, who go about it as enthusiastically as we do, if not more so. Master of ceremonies was Pasang Nima, known as the Pocket Rocket due to his size and energy. Rarely did I see him without a bottle of Khukri Rum in his hand, ready to swoop. Three shots – an auspicious number in Buddhism – were obligatory each time we were caught. Despite having a tin of Tuborg in my hand I was caught three times in the first half hour, which meant nine shots. Next came the chang, a milky fluid that tastes like weak beer. I was happy to give it a miss, but when I saw Margaret and Edita each take three large mugfuls in quick succession I knew I was in trouble. Although I hid behind a rock, the Pocket Rocket soon found me. This part of the ceremony lasted rather longer than the chanting, and it was best summed up by Peter, a 61-year-old attorney from Idaho who was climbing with the Junkies for the first time. 'I can't remember the last time I was drunk before noon,' he later said.

We spent the next few days resting and acclimatising. Our communications failed this year, and our comms tent, with its array of laptops, remained unvisited. The BGAN/Inmarsat satellite connection didn't work at all; the NCell 3G cell-phone connection stopped working from the moment the Asian Trekking team arrived at base camp and erected a huge satellite dish. Several members of the team made frequent visits to the teahouses of Gorak Shep, an hour's walk away, where there was Wi-Fi connectivity. These trips were invariably exhausting, but good exercise. The reason for this was the large number of base camp trekkers clogging up the trail at their unusual walking pace, akin to that of an asthmatic tortoise. The trail between Gorak Shep and base camp undulates quite a lot to begin with, and it was usual for us to encounter a long line of trekkers on the uphill sections. Never once did they move out of the way, so we had to boulder-hop beside the trail at a canter in order to get past. On one occasion Margaret – 64-year-old Supergran who has summited Everest from both the north and south sides – arrived back at camp and exclaimed: 'Oh my god, I nearly killed a trekker!' In fact, the trekker in question nearly killed himself after deciding that being overtaken by a 64-year-old grandmother was something he couldn't handle. He chased after her and took the lead again before collapsing in a wheezing heap at the top of a rise. Margaret sauntered past him for a second time.

THE WORLD'S MOST EXPENSIVE EVEREST BASE CAMP TREK

Then came that fateful day, 18 April, which will forever be one of the darkest days in Everest history. That morning we decided to go for our first foray into the Khumbu Icefall. Our Sherpas had been up twice already doing load carries, most recently the day before; they reported that the ladders weren't as safe as they should be and needed fixing. We decided to postpone a visit to Camp 1 until this was done, but it was time we started to do some climbing. Instead of leaving at 3am – usual for a first visit to the icefall – and climbing all the way to Camp 1, we set off later, intending to climb for just a couple of hours to give ourselves a workout. On such slender decisions are lives lost or saved.

At approximately 6.45am, we were walking through Everest Base Camp when a huge chunk of ice fell off Everest's West Shoulder, triggering an avalanche that swept across the entire width of the icefall.

We were very lucky. Had we set off two hours earlier we may well have been swept away. Others weren't so lucky. There were as many as 100 people in the Khumbu Icefall that morning. How many were trapped by the avalanche we didn't know, but it soon became clear that a major tragedy was unfolding before our eyes.

In fact, the catastrophe could hardly have happened at a worse time, or in a worse location. A ladder had fallen out of position at a steep section of the route through the icefall, causing a bottleneck. At that moment, 40 or 50 Sherpas were standing above the ladder in the path of the avalanche, waiting to come down. Many were killed instantly – not by being buried, but from shards of shattered ice exploding like shrapnel. Injuries were horrific. Many survivors and rescuers were traumatised by what they saw.

Shortly after the avalanche we arrived at the foot of the Khumbu Icefall and peered up into the ice through our cameras. We were relieved to see many little figures –

survivors – still up there on the ice. We did not know then how many had been killed, but over the next few hours the true picture began to emerge.

Somewhere near the skyline we could see figures trapped above the fallen ladder and gingerly edging their way down. They were very close to the West Shoulder where the serac had fallen.

Those who were already acclimatised to the altitude, including Sherpas and western guides, headed up to the avalanche site. Some took ladders to restore the route; others took spades to help retrieve the fallen. At around 10am, helicopters began arriving to bring down the dead and injured to base camp. An emergency room had been set up at the Himalayan Rescue Association's Everest Base Camp medical clinic.

Crowds gathered at the helipads and watched in disbelief as one by one the deceased were brought down on long lines. The helicopters returned again and again. We lost count of the number of journeys they made.

In all 16 people died that day. It could have been anybody – a team of western clients from International Mountain Guides (IMG) were climbing through the icefall at the time and just 15 minutes away from the tragedy – but it so happened that all of the dead came from Nepal. While not all teams lost members, all of us had those who were friends or family of the dead.

Edita returned to camp in tears after learning that Dorje Khatri, who had been with her on the summit of Cho Oyu, was one of them. Dorje Khatri was also the cousin of Ang Gelu, who was up there helping to dig out the bodies. Even now I struggle to find the words to convey our sense of shock.

Darker events unfolded before dinner. We were settling down to eat when we heard noisy voices outside the tent.

Robert and Phil went out to investigate, and saw a mob of about 30 Sherpas passing through camp.

'What's going on?' Robert said.

'It's nothing,' Phil replied.

'Don't lie to me.'

It was the start of the troubles – threats, intimidation and eventually a full-blown Sherpa strike – that would unravel over the coming week. Our Sherpas had no desire to join the mob. Wise and experienced sirdar that he is, Dorje sent two of our team to walk with them and make a show of solidarity.

Later that evening a wonderful thing happened. I was on my way back to my tent after dinner when Phil emerged from the Sherpa dining tent, a place that is usually out of bounds to us clients.

'Hey, Mark, come in here – the Sherpas would like us to join them tonight.'

I went inside to find all my teammates mingling with our crew of 30 Sherpas. Rum and Tuborg was being passed around and they squeezed up to make room for me. Despite the horrors of the day, they were all smiling. Phil introduced the four new Junkies clients – Jay, Peter, Caroline and Ricardo – and for the next hour we were able to enjoy ourselves in spite of the events engulfing base camp. I don't know whose idea it was to have this impromptu party on the night of a major tragedy, whether Phil's or Dorje's or most likely both of them, but in the context of events that were to follow it became significant.

The week that followed felt like a year. Some day someone will probably write a book about the twists and turns and politics that swallowed up the tragedy and made it seem insignificant, if only for a while. Despite the headlines about Everest being a walk, it will always be dangerous, and all of us who climb it accept a level of risk that seems difficult to understand for those who don't. When tragedy happens, every climber makes a personal decision to call a halt or keep climbing. Some feel that to carry on is disrespectful; others feel that were they to die themselves they would want their teammates to continue and ensure their struggles were not in vain. There is no right or wrong answer to this dilemma. It should really be a decision for the individual.

We expected a period of mourning to follow, then perhaps another puja to appease the mountain gods. We were lucky in the Altitude Junkies team. We had lost no one and all of us, client and Sherpa alike, wanted to keep climbing. But events were overtaking us as a handful of militant Sherpas from other teams agitated for an end to the season. The politics were complex. On 20 April a petition was handed to MoCTCA containing a number of demands. These included better compensation for the families of the Sherpas who had died, expenses for the injured, a relief fund for future accidents, better insurance and cover for helicopter evacuation, an immediate end to the climbing season with full pay to staff, and helicopters to bring equipment down from the Western Cwm. It was a strange form of labour dispute. Instead of 'these are our conditions or we go on strike', it was 'here are our conditions *and* we go on strike *and* you must pay us'. Many of the demands were reasonable, but all of them? How was that going to work? There would be many more losers than there needed to be. None of the Junkies Sherpas signed the petition.

On 22 April we watched a puja for the dead turn into a political rally. I was appalled. Western leaders were invited to speak, and they did the only appropriate thing under the circumstances by saying a few words for those who had died and nothing more. The militants were less scrupulous and the movement to keep climbing was losing momentum.

Stories started emerging about threats and intimidation to Sherpas who wished to keep working. There were rumours that threats had been made against clients from Himex. That evening Phil took a helicopter to Kathmandu with Himex's owner, Russell Brice, for a meeting with officials from MoCTCA to see if he could persuade them to take urgent action to keep the season going.

On 23 April I escaped the base camp politics and joined Kevin and Edita for a walk to Camp 1 on Pumori, a notable viewpoint an hour or so above camp where we were told you could see right up into the Western Cwm. It was cloudy but we were pleased to be doing what we came here to do: to climb high and enjoy the lovely mountain scenery. We were still hopeful that we would get our opportunity; some teams, those who had lost Sherpas, were going home, but enough of us remained to fix the route and continue with our expeditions. Three teams – ourselves, Himex and Asian Trekking – all intended to stay; and although the biggest team on the mountain, IMG, didn't seem quite as committed, they were still here too. We were relaxed and happy, and as we ascended the flanks of Pumori, Lhotse gradually began to rise into view above the Khumbu Icefall. It was still wreathed in cloud when we arrived at Camp 1, and Everest was completely obscured, but the rest of the view was clear – and immense. We could see right across the Lho La to the North Col, from where Edita and I had both taken our journeys to the summit. On the other side we could see all the way down the Khumbu Glacier to a panorama of peaks, including Ama Dablam, Kangtega and Taboche, and the skies were gradually clearing. Everest's summit emerged just as some South African members of the Asian Trekking team joined us at the viewpoint. Were the mountain gods smiling on us at last? We returned to base camp full of hope.

As the most responsible member of the team, Robert had

been left in charge in Phil's absence. During happy hour he put us on speakerphone for a conversation with our leader back in Kathmandu. Phil was upbeat about his meeting that day. Officials from MoCTCA, including the Minister of Tourism himself, had assured him and Russell they would agree to most of the Sherpa demands, provide icefall doctors to maintain the climbing route through the icefall, put pressure on the Sherpas to return to work by threatening bans for those who refused, and send army troops to base camp to provide protection for those who wished to continue working. A delegation would also fly into base camp tomorrow to announce the terms. It all sounded positive, and as it was happy hour we decided to take advantage of Phil's absence and Robert's good nature by ordering more wine than we would normally drink. Ricardo, a musician by trade, entertained us with some singing. But the evening ended in despondency when we received a visit from a friend of Caroline's who was a client with IMG. He told us that his team had been instructed to pack their things and leave base camp tomorrow. It was a shock. IMG were the biggest team on the mountain, with experienced Sherpas capable of taking on a large share of the rope fixing. If they joined ourselves, Himex and Asian Trekking, then we knew the mountain could still be climbed. But fixing the route all the way to the summit of Everest is a massive task; without IMG, the burden would fall heavily on the Sherpas of the three remaining teams. Would we be enough?

It was a forlorn figure who emerged alone from the helicopter the following morning, 24 April, and walked into camp. We watched Phil trudge wearily from the helipad and approach our tents. Although his meeting had gone well, the news about IMG had been a major blow and he was taking it hard. It must have seemed that nobody else cared about remaining on the mountain.

THE WORLD'S MOST EXPENSIVE EVEREST BASE CAMP TREK

The farce of a meeting that followed ended any hope of climbing. Flying into base camp at an altitude of 5,270m is a risky business. Those who weren't acclimatised would need to start breathing supplementary oxygen from the moment they stepped out of the helicopter, and it wouldn't be safe to remain there long. Whatever business they needed to conduct would therefore need to be quick and efficient.

Hundreds were gathered outside the tents of the Sagarmatha Pollution Control Committee (SPCC) where the meeting was taking place: an equal spread of westerners and Sherpas. But first, the delegation disappeared inside a tent for omelette, garlic soup and pancakes. The speeches that followed were conducted entirely in Nepali with no translation into English, so most of us didn't have a clue what was being said, but after a while it became clear that the militants were getting the upper hand. I didn't wait for the end. Instead I walked back to the Junkies camp knowing that the season was over. I have no reason to doubt what Phil said about his meeting with the ministry; of all the things they told him they would do, the only one they actually did was fly to base camp. Still, I hope the garlic soup was tasty and worth the journey.

The following day, 25 April, our liaison officer showed up at base camp. She had brought her husband with her and looked exhausted after the trek, but where had she been when we needed her? In any case she was not a Sherpa and didn't look like she travelled much in the mountains – perhaps not the ideal person to handle the delicate negotiations associated with expedition work. Dorje was furious with her.

The next day we trekked down to Pheriche to board helicopters. On the evening of 26 April most of us were back in Kathmandu precisely 23 days after leaving, having got only as far as base camp. As Everest Base Camp treks go, it had been expensive. I was on a Lhotse permit, so mine was one of the cheaper ones; it had cost me only US$20,000. Our Everest team mates had paid over $40,000 for the same trip, and Altitude Junkies run one of the cheaper expeditions. Many of the things we had paid for – permit fees, government liaison officer fee, icefall doctor and rope-fixing fees, costs for food, fuel and oxygen for the rest of the expedition – were gone. Phil agreed to pay all of our Sherpas in full and none of us objected. They had stood by us throughout the expedition and had been as keen to climb as we were. They have families to support, and why should they suffer for something that was not their fault? But for us westerners, this was the year of the world's most expensive Everest Base Camp trek.

This is a trip report and I have therefore provided the perspective of a commercial client. Of course, I haven't talked about some of the wider issues associated with this season. These have been covered extensively elsewhere, but little by me so far. When we arrived back in Kathmandu we were besieged by journalists keen for us to help them with their stories. Some of my teammates agreed to talk, but I chose not to. This wasn't because I have nothing to say, but because I was still in a state of shock; I knew it would take me a while to make sense of it all, and I didn't want a journalist to take my words and interpret them for me. Perhaps only four men and a dog read this blog and the media would provide a wider audience, but at least these are my words.

I still have plenty more to say and I intend to say it over the next few weeks. I'm sorry for those of you who are bored with Everest, but there are other blogs and I hope you will come back again later in the year.

THE WORLD'S MOST EXPENSIVE EVEREST BASE CAMP TREK

This post is dedicated to the 16 who died in the Khumbu Icefall this year, and all the Sherpas who work the high mountains. We couldn't do it without them.

- Mingma Nuru Sherpa, *Shangri-La*
- Dorji Sherpa, *Shangri-La*
- Ang Tshiri Sherpa, *Shangri-La*
- Tenzing Chottar Sherpa, *Shangri-La*
- Nima Sherpa, *Shangri-La*
- Phurba Ongyal Sherpa, *Himalayan Guides*
- Lakpa Tenjing Sherpa, *Himalayan Guides*
- Chhiring Ongchu Sherpa, *Himalayan Guides*
- Dorjee Khatri, *Himalayan Guides*
- Then Dorjee Sherpa, *Himalayan Guides*
- Phur Temba Sherpa, *Himalayan Guides*
- Pasang Karma Sherpa, *Summit Trekking*
- Asman Tamang, *Himalayan Ecstasy*
- Angkaji Sherpa, *Seven Summit Treks*
- Ash Bahadur Gurung, *Seven Summit Treks*
- Pemba Tenji Sherpa, *Seven Summit Treks*

Puja-cum-protest at Everest base camp in 2014.

12
THE EVEREST BASE CAMP SUMMIT MEETING: AN EYEWITNESS ACCOUNT

29 May 2014

On 24 April a delegation of government officials flew to Everest Base Camp by helicopter to meet with Sherpas who had issued demands following a fatal avalanche on 18 April. Afterwards the government issued a press release that was misleading in a number of ways, and which contradicted the outcome concluded by those of us who attended. Here is my account of the events I witnessed that day.

Two days after an avalanche in the Khumbu Icefall killed 16 Sherpas, the government announced compensation of 40,000 Nepalese rupees (around US$400) for each of the families of the victims. With permit fees of $10,000 per climber going into government coffers, the amount offered was seen as derisory by the Sherpa community, and this galvanised a number of militant Sherpas into issuing a petition to the government containing several demands. These included additional compensation for the families of victims of the avalanche, setting up a trust fund for victims of future accidents, and better insurance for Sherpas. They also included a right to abandon their expeditions with full pay – a demand that could only be fulfilled with the agreement of western operators and their clients. While backing many of the demands, most westerners and some Sherpas wished to remain on the mountain and continue with their expeditions. The aim of the summit meeting was to reach an agreement that would satisfy most of the Sherpa demands while enabling expeditions to continue.

The full list of demands was as follows:

- Increment of immediate relief announced for avalanche victims
- Provide 1 million rupees each to families of deceased
- Set up a memorial park in the name of the deceased in Kathmandu
- Cover all expenses for treatment of the injured
- Provide 1 million rupees to critically hurt who cannot rejoin mountaineering activities
- Set up mountaineering relief fund with 30 per cent of royalty collected from issuing permits to different mountains
- Double the insurance amount to the mountaineering workers
- Provide additional chopper rescue to mountaineering support staff if insurance fails to cover the cost
- Provide perks and salaries, except summit bonus, through concerned agencies to Sherpas if they want to call off climbing this season
- Manage chopper to bring logistics and equipment from different camps if mountaineers decide to abandon climbing this season
- Don't take action against SPCC icefall doctors if they refuse to fix ropes and ladders on the route this season

THE EVEREST BASE CAMP SUMMIT MEETING

- Let the expedition members call off this season's climbing if they wish to[29]

After the meeting, the Ministry of Tourism issued a press release implying that they had talked with both operators and Sherpas, that they'd gained the agreement of all parties (guides, climbers and 'other concerned people') to continue with their expeditions, and that the mountain was therefore still open. Along with many other westerners I was a witness at that meeting, and I left it under no illusions that the season was now over. The press release issued by the Ministry of Tourism was disingenuous, misleading, and largely fictional.

It was about 9am when several helicopters arrived with various officials from the government and tourist industry in Nepal, and I hurried over to the tents of the Sagarmatha Pollution Control Committee (SPCC), where the meeting was due to take place. Earlier in the week this had been the location for a puja for the dead that had been hijacked by militants and turned into a political rally. Half a dozen chairs had been set out in front of one of the tents where the ground sloped away to a trough in the moraine of the glacier. In front of the chairs were several large boulders that people were standing on to watch, and behind these a sizeable mound of moraine formed a kind of grandstand providing a view of the proceedings for around 100 people. I would estimate that there were 200–300 people in total watching the meeting; there seemed to be an equal spread of Sherpas and westerners. I managed to find a space on one of the rocks where some of my teammates were gathered.

We did not expect the meeting to last for long. The delegation was flying in from Kathmandu, at an altitude of 1,400m, to base camp at 5,270m. Most would not be acclimatised and would need to breathe supplementary oxygen from the moment they stepped out of the helicopter. Even with this, it would not be safe for them to remain at that altitude for long.

The delegation reached the SPCC tents at 9.15am and immediately disappeared inside one of them, leaving the chairs that had been set out for our benefit empty. Several people who had been milling around outside this tent entered it with the delegation, including some of the known militants. I don't remember seeing any westerners follow them in. For the first half hour the rest of us saw nothing of what went on, but watched in disbelief as trays of pancake, omelette, Tibetan bread, tea and soup were taken in. With not a moment to lose and the livelihoods of hundreds of Sherpas and expedition operators – as well as the hopes and dreams of an equal number of western climbers who had invested tens of thousands of dollars to be here – dependent on the outcome of this meeting, were the government officials taking *breakfast?* It seemed incredibly disrespectful to those of us who had paid for all these people to be here.

At around 9.45am the delegation emerged from the tent. Everyone crowded around to take photographs as the most important members of the delegation took chairs; others who emerged from the tent, including some of the militants, sat on the ground behind them. An earnest-looking man in a blue jacket then stood up to make a speech. He was not introduced to the crowd, though I believe he may have been a representative of the Nepal National Mountain Guides Association (NNMGA), the body who regulate official UIAGM/IFMGA mountain guide qualifications in Nepal. He looked honest, and projected his voice so that everyone could hear clearly, but he spoke entirely in Nepali. After ten minutes he finished speaking and half the audience clapped politely. The other half assumed that someone would translate the speech into English, but it didn't happen.

Instead, a second man in an orange down jacket and Nepali topi hat stood up and launched into another speech.

Where the first man spoke solemnly, this second man spoke more passionately. Although he was not introduced, our climbing sirdar later told me that he was Ramesh Dhamala, president of the Trekking Agencies' Association of Nepal (TAAN), the trade body representing trekking operators in Nepal. Although he spoke in Nepali it was evident to all that his words didn't appeal to the militants. Several of them stood up from their positions behind the delegation and started moving around, gesticulating furiously and inciting other people in the crowd. Most prominent among these agitators was Pasang Tenzing Sherpa, sirdar with the British mountaineering company Jagged Globe.[30] Was the speaker telling them they had to go back to work, that if they didn't it would do great damage to Nepal's tourism industry? Was he reminding them that the trekking industry extends throughout Nepal, and by going on strike they would harm other people in poorer parts of the country? Whatever he was saying it was clear they didn't like it, but we never found out, because his speech also wasn't translated, and as far as I'm aware there are no transcripts available.

A third man stood up and delivered a less impassioned speech. Again he was not introduced, but I believe he was Ang Tshering Sherpa: president of the Nepal Mountaineering Association (NMA), the organisation responsible for Nepal's trekking peaks, and owner of Asian Trekking, one of the few teams on the mountain whose Sherpas had not signed the petition. Again he spoke in Nepali and received polite applause.

Until now it had been hard to gauge the mood of the meeting or the direction it was heading, but, apart from a few excited agitators during the second speech, there was nothing to indicate pressure was being exerted on the militants to return to work, or that concessions had been made to meet the Sherpa demands. It was disappointing that with so many western climbers present who stood to lose a great deal if the season were abandoned – and who had paid tens of thousands of dollars into the pockets of many of the people gathered there and collectively put millions into the Nepalese economy – nobody considered it important enough to translate the speeches into English.

The meeting took a turn for the worse when Pasang Bhote, one of the leaders of the militants, stood up, turned his back on the crowd, and instead addressed the delegation. I have been unable to discover which operator Pasang Bhote was working for this year, but believe it may have been the SPCC itself: the public body responsible for employing the icefall doctors who fix and maintain the route through the Khumbu Icefall. It was Pasang Bhote who had been most prominent at the puja earlier in the week that militants turned into a political rally. I believe he may be some form of mountain workers' union leader. Today he spoke passionately at the government officials, occasionally receiving whoops of delight from some of the Sherpas gathered in the crowd. Again, I had no idea what was being said, but I didn't like it. The atmosphere in the crowd did not seem aggressive, but all the westerners were keeping silent, and I had the feeling that if anyone interrupted then things could change very quickly. Just like the puja it was beginning to feel to me as if the meeting had been hijacked by the militants and turned into a rally.

At 10.30am it was clear which way the tide was heading. I no longer had the will to stand on a rock and listen as people stuck a knife into my hopes and dreams in a language I didn't understand. I stepped down and trudged wearily back to our campsite, utterly dejected and knowing my expedition was over before we had even begun to climb.

The final act of the drama was described to me when other members of the team returned to camp. Shortly after 11 o'clock, as I rested in my tent pondering the events leading to this, I heard a distant rumble followed by a loud cheer much closer to where I lay. Everyone had left the SPCC tents and followed the delegation to the helipad near to our camp. Just as some of them were boarding their helicopter, another chunk of ice broke off the West Shoulder in exactly the same location as the one that had triggered the fatal avalanche. It was not as big an avalanche this time, but still it billowed across the same bit of climbing route through the Khumbu Icefall. The sun was up and warming the ice. It was much too late for anyone to be climbing through the icefall had the route been open, but nevertheless the timing of this event felt like a clear sign from on high.

There was a time not so long ago when Sherpas were superstitious folk who believed the mountains to be the abode of mountain gods. Perhaps some still are. Every expedition begins with a puja to appease the gods and ask for safe passage. But the cheer I heard as I lay in my tent was not the awed gratitude of superstitious people who had received a warning from the gods. This was the cheer of folk who were young and cynical, who don't believe in mountain gods any more than we do. But we all knew what the avalanche meant this time. The militants had won the battle and we should all go home. It was over.

Now that you have read my account of the meeting, here is the text of the government's press release. Have a read and let me know if you think it's describing the same event:

Today, one high level delegation headed by Hon'ble minister for Culture, Tourism and Civil Aviation Bhim Prasad Acharya had visited the Mount Everest Base Camp and seriously discussed with mountain guide, supporting climbers and other concerned people. The delegation comprised with representatives of different tourism related organizations.

During the discussion, the minister had urged to continue the expedition activities to all team leaders and members and requested to all concerned agencies to fix ladder & rope. At the time the supporting climbers also agreed to support expedition activities.

However, if some expedition team wants to quit the expedition for this season and request to ministry to extend their permit, the ministry would make necessary process to extend the time of their permit for next five years for the expedition team of 2014 spring.

Here, the ministry strongly request to all the expedition team to continue the expedition because they have made all the required arrangement for completion of their expedition.[31]

I didn't see any discussions with mountain guides and 'other concerned people'. It was all in Nepali and we were excluded. I certainly didn't see any supporting climbers (i.e. Sherpas) agreeing to support expedition activities. On the contrary, they cheered to see that the season was over. The minister may have requested concerned agencies to fix ladder and rope, but in reality the icefall doctors weren't fixing anything – and until they did none of us could climb.

As for making all the required arrangements for the completion of expeditions, what was required was for the government to agree to the more reasonable of the Sherpa demands: more compensation for families, a trust fund and better insurance. The army needed to be sent to base camp to restore order and provide protection for any Sherpas who wished to continue working, including the icefall doctors. Police were needed to remove from base camp those who had threatened violence against other Sherpas and their families. Expedition leaders had met with government officials in Kathmandu the day before and explained these requirements to them. The officials promised these things would happen. Without them the ministry could request all it liked for expeditions to continue, but they would not be able to.

None of this was resolved at the meeting. The government's press release was a work of fiction. Most tragic of all is that 16 brave men died in an avalanche, and their families will need to rely on the generosity of westerners for support. And while their deaths had the potential to do good, by being the catalyst that leads to better and safer working conditions for their community, it has so far done nothing of the sort. It has led to divisive political activism that will likely keep people away from Nepal and make it harder for the community to find well-paid work. The government could have prevented this, but they failed. Then they lied about it.

13
LEO HOULDING DOES HIS BIT FOR THE SHERPAS

11 June 2014

I was tapping away on my keyboard last Thursday when a friend reminded me that one of Britain's premier rock climbers was doing a lecture at the Royal Geographical Society in London that evening. Rock climbing isn't generally my thing unless there's a fixed rope to haul myself up on, but this particular lecture had an Everest theme. It was being sponsored by the Himalayan Trust (the charity Sir Edmund Hillary set up to build schools and hospitals in the Khumbu region of Nepal) and one of the aims of the evening was to raise money for the families of the Sherpas who died in the 18 April avalanche in the Khumbu Icefall. Leo Houlding had flown in especially from a climbing trip to Colorado to give the talk. So, this week I'm going to be making a rare foray into the world of big-wall rock climbing, an activity that frankly terrifies me, and not any less so after hearing this lecture.

We probably weren't Leo's usual audience of young and thrusting hardcore rock-climbing enthusiasts. Most seemed to be older folk; friends of Nepal, perhaps, who had supported the Himalayan Trust after many happy visits to the country. Apart from Leo himself (who turned up dressed in a pair of knee-length shorts) I appeared to be one of the youngest people there, and it was far from being the sell-out you might expect for such a high-profile and charismatic speaker. He started by asking how many people in the audience were rock climbers, and whether we understood terms like 'E5' and 'off width'. A few hands went up, but I expect he concluded that he would need to talk in plain English.

He talked about two of his most heavily publicised climbs, both of which were made into films. The second of these was his ascent of an enormous piece of rock in Queen Maud Land, Antarctica, called Ulvetanna. It's quite a scary rock climb and I was in danger of soiling my underpants just watching the trailer – which, given that I was sitting on the balcony and there were people below me, would not have been cool.

Of more interest to me was the first part of Leo's talk. In 2007 he travelled to the north side of Everest with the American climber Conrad Anker as part of the team making the film *The Wildest Dream* about George Mallory and Sandy Irvine's disappearance in 1924. They wanted to find out whether it were possible for the pair to have free climbed the Second Step, and the idea was that the more experienced Conrad would play Mallory with the younger Leo playing the climbing greenhorn Irvine. It was a nice idea in theory, but it had a basic flaw. Before Irvine went to Everest the only climbing he had done was a spot of pootling in Spitsbergen. By contrast, although Leo was a newcomer to extreme altitude in 2007, he was already one of the world's leading rock climbers and was capable of dancing up the Second Step in the style of a tango.

Despite this, Leo concluded that Mallory and Irvine

probably didn't get up the Second Step.

'I would rate it as HVS,' he said, 'or Hard Very Severe,' which he presumably added for the benefit of any gynaecologists in the audience who thought it stood for High Vaginal Swab. 'I've done most of Mallory's climbs in the Alps, and most of them were HVS too, so he was definitely capable of climbing it, but it's a different story at that altitude.'

The final part of the evening, and its main purpose, was the fundraising. This year it had a theme that was very close to my heart.

Compère Rebecca Stephens, who became the first British woman to climb Everest in 1993 and is now chair of the Himalayan Trust UK, showed us a film of the late Sir Edmund Hillary and his friend and Everest teammate George Lowe, who died in 2013, visiting schools in the Khumbu region of Nepal that have been built and funded by the charity.

'Hillary, Hillary,' the kids were chanting as they arrived.

'It's not the mountains but the people who keep us coming back here,' George Lowe said to his friend as they walked along a trail.

He is not alone in that feeling. Hundreds of trekkers and climbers visit the Everest region every year. They return home retaining a huge amount of goodwill for the Sherpas who have helped them to achieve their dreams, and they resolve to help out by donating to charities like the Himalayan Trust.

Rebecca then introduced us to Ang Jangbu Sherpa, an inspirational figure who attended one of Sir Edmund Hillary's schools as a child but dreamed of becoming a helicopter pilot. While working in the trekking industry as a young man he was lucky to have caught the attention of a wealthy trekker who took him under his wing and sponsored him to visit the United States and train to be a pilot. He graduated with flying colours (literally) and is now a commercial airline pilot who flies Boeing 747s.

He shuffled onto the stage and quietly explained that he's not used to public speaking in front of so many people, but agreed to talk because the 18 April avalanche left many families back home bereaved and deprived of their main breadwinner. He explained that Sherpas in the Khumbu region are familiar with death in climbing accidents; while they knew that such events couldn't be prevented on Everest, after the avalanche the Sherpas got together and demanded better insurance cover so that families of the victims could be provided for. He explained that they were not striking for better wages, but for greater security.

While this may be true, it occurred to me that, having observed Sherpa militancy first hand, I was perhaps the only person in the audience who had lost some of my goodwill for the Sherpas following the avalanche and its aftermath instead of having gained it. I was invited to the lecture by a friend of mine who has recently become a trustee of the Himalayan Trust UK. As a trustee of a charity operating in Nepal myself, I was intrigued how he came to be involved with such a prestigious one as this, and had a chat with him about it before the lecture. Outside the entrance they were selling tickets for a raffle for the victims' families. My friend appeared to be embarrassed when I put my hand in my pocket and produced a fiver.

'No, honestly Mark, don't feel you have to buy a ticket. You've spent enough already,' he said.

He was right in a way: I invested the best part of $20,000 in the Khumbu region this year to pay for my expedition to Lhotse, which was cut short by the Sherpa strike – but another £5 wasn't going to break the bank if it went to someone who needed it more than me. I admitted that, when people have asked me which of the many charities raising funds for the avalanche victims they should donate to, I have directed them to the Himalayan Trust because of their long history of building schools and hospitals for the Sherpas. You can be sure that money you donate to them will be spent wisely.

But I believe it's also important to put things in perspective. Since the avalanche Sherpas have been presented as an exploited underclass who have been treated poorly by uncaring westerners in pursuit of Everest glory. This is a distortion of the true picture by people who are unaware of Sherpa history, and how closely their increasing prosperity over the last 100 years has been inextricably linked to mountaineering expeditions. The Sherpas of this generation may be Everest guides, but their children are the doctors, teachers and airline pilots of tomorrow. Much of this is due to the schools and hospitals that organisations like the Himalayan Trust have built, and because of the generosity of westerners such as the one who paid for Ang Jangbu's flying lessons, but most of all it is because of income generated by the tourism industry. The trekking industry has grown out of the mountaineering expeditions that first visited Nepal. Many Sherpas are now teahouse owners or have their own trekking and climbing agencies. Climbing Sherpas are paid comparatively generous salaries, which enable them to send their children to good schools. And, as more Sherpas find opportunities outside of mountaineering, other ethnic groups, such as Tamangs and Gurungs, are starting to fill the vacancies. This is progress. It benefits everyone.

Organisations like the Himalayan Trust, and the Sherpa community themselves, should be wary of the militant tendency that emerged this year and hope that it doesn't spread into trekking and other parts of the tourist industry.

LEO HOULDING DOES HIS BIT FOR THE SHERPAS

If this happens then in future it's likely that I won't be the only person in the audience watching the romantic and heart-warming speeches with one eyebrow raised. However small the problem may be now, a new generation of Sherpas is emerging who are in danger of eroding the goodwill and generosity of westerners who care about Nepal by being more combative. For example, I saw one Sherpa complain on his Facebook page that he didn't receive his summit bonus this year. In many ways the direction of movement is positive. You could say the Himalayan Trust are building schools for people who are rapidly taking control of their own destiny, and the most successful charities are those who become obsolete because the people they support are no longer dependent. But this greater control needs to be used constructively. Of course, Ang Jangbu didn't mention the Sherpas who threatened to break the legs of other Sherpas if they didn't go on strike.

Another important point to raise is that a disproportionate amount of charity goes to the Khumbu region and Sherpas who are relatively wealthy compared to people in other parts of Nepal. A great deal – in excess of $700,000 – has been raised for Sherpa families already. In the immediate aftermath of the tragedy many appeals and trust funds were set up to raise money for those who had lost family members. For example, the Chinese climbers Quingyong Zhang and Geng Zhu, part of the Everest Chinese Dream Expedition team who lost Sherpas in the avalanche, pledged 7 million Nepalese rupees (around $70,000) to the families of the victims. A fund set up by the American Alpine Club had raised $50,000 before the end of April. The Japanese climber Ken Noguchi announced that he would be making a donation of 10 million yen (about $97,000). A GoFundMe page for the families of three Sherpas employed by Himalayan Guides aims to raise $50,000 and is well on the way. By the middle of May, the New Zealand branch of the Himalayan Trust had themselves raised NZ$29,000 (around US$25,000). *National Geographic* photographer Aaron Huey raised an astonishing $424,000 by selling prints over the course of eight days.

Many newspaper and magazine reports have described how dangerous the work of a climbing Sherpa is compared to other jobs, but 16 deaths this year in a freak act of nature does not even remotely compare to the 400 Nepalis who have been reported to have died in Qatar building stadiums for the 2022 World Cup.[32] Climbing Sherpas can earn as much as $5,000 in the two-month period they work on Everest. This may not sound much to westerners living in an expensive city like London, but it goes a long way in a country where the gross national income per capita is believed to be around $700. Most Nepalis don't have the option of becoming climbing Sherpas. Thousands travel to the Middle East to work in the construction industry and send money back to their families. There are plenty of horror stories and the Qatar World Cup is merely the highest-profile one.

Climbing Sherpas have to contend with some risk – as indeed do all Everest climbers – but they earn a good wage for their country and many of their children have much greater opportunities. I would certainly encourage you to donate to organisations like the Himalayan Trust that support the Sherpas. I owe a great many happy memories to them. Having watched the avalanche come down with my own eyes as I made my way into the icefall that morning, and then seen the bodies airlifted out, I can't help thinking about the sacrifice those innocent people made and the great void left behind for their friends and family.

Anyway, I'm conscious that, like the puja for the dead at Everest Base Camp this year that was hijacked by militant

Sherpas and turned into a political rally, I've hijacked this post about a lecture by Leo Houlding in support of the Himalayan Trust and turned it into a rant of my own. It remains for me to tell you about the raffle. There were some great prizes, including a print signed by not only Sir Edmund Hillary but Tenzing Norgay as well (how on earth they managed this when he died in 1986 heaven only knows), a book signed by Sir Edmund Hillary, and a DVD signed by Leo Houlding.

'It's a bit crap compared to the other prizes,' Leo said with a sheepish chuckle as this was read out.

I would happily have won Leo's DVD, but whatever – it had been an enjoyable and successful evening, well worth the price of my entrance fee and raffle tickets.

14
THE COD SCIENCE OF EVEREST HATE

25 June 2014

One of the things every Everest climber has to get used to sooner or later is hate written about them in the media. I first discovered this when I came back from Everest in 2012, and found it so extreme that I ended up writing a response that is still one of my most popular blog posts.[33] Of course, I could have just ignored the insults, and usually I do because life's too short. The primary ingredient of hate is ignorance. If people choose to be ignorant, generally that's a problem for them rather than me.

Every so often, however, the hate becomes so pervasive that it starts to resemble propaganda. Propaganda thrives on ignorance, and those who use it hope that if they say something enough times without it being corrected then it will eventually be treated as fact even if it's not true. I'm reaching the end of my series of posts about this year's Everest season and it's probably starting to look like I have a chip on my shoulder. If this is the case then I apologise; but I believe that one or two more things need to be said in a last effort to stop ignorance becoming too deep-rooted, and then I will move onto other topics, I promise.

The theory that Sherpas are helpless serfs who are ruthlessly exploited by selfish westerners is one such popular misconception promoted in the media that is starting to look like a propaganda campaign. It is a campaign based on ignorance of Sherpa history, overlooking the fact that mountaineering, and the trekking industry that grew from it, have provided Sherpas with greater opportunities and enabled them to become wealthy by Nepali standards. I talked in a little more detail about this previously – the simple fact is, mountaineering and trekking and the work they bring have been good for the Sherpa community; and while their working conditions can certainly be improved – and regularly are being – unless this basic premise is recognised, the propaganda will ultimately harm rather than help them.

One particularly corrosive piece of propaganda that has appeared frequently in the media since the 18 April avalanche is the notion that being a climbing Sherpa on Everest is 12 times more deadly than being a US soldier during the Iraq war. In the last couple of months this 'fact' has appeared in publications as diverse as *The Guardian*,[34] *Business Insider*,[35] the *Washington Post*,[36] *Al Jazeera*[37] and a website called, curiously, *Live Science* (which appears to use the word 'science' in its loosest sense).[38] All of these publications appear to have used the same source, but not one of them questioned how that source came by this figure, or suggested in any way that it might be suspect. In the scientific community, if such a statistic were to be quoted as fact it would need to come from a reputable source, and be backed up by hard data and sound methodology that had been subject to rigorous peer review. None of these requirements have been met.

So what was the source? The statistics supporting this assertion were originally published in an article by *Outside* magazine on 18 April, the very day of the avalanche in the Khumbu Icefall that killed 16 Sherpas.[39] *Outside* magazine had originally asserted that being an Everest climbing Sherpa was over three and half times more dangerous than being a US soldier,[40] but by including the fatalities from the 18 April avalanche in their data they were able to up this to 12 times more dangerous (in the same way that if they had conducted the research around the period 11 September 2001 they would have been able to conclude that being a New York office worker was at least as dangerous as being a gatekeeper in Samarkand as Genghis Khan's Mongol hordes were sweeping across Central Asia).

So much for the source; how did they arrive at their conclusion? I'm neither a scientist nor a statistician, but I do recognise shoddy research when it tattoos itself with the words 'shoddy research' and dances provocatively in front of me. My critique is a little limited compared to what you would get from a proper scientist, but hopefully there is enough here to convince you that *Outside* magazine has a few questions to answer before this particular piece of propaganda is spread any further.

The article starts by showing a nice neat table recording the number of deaths in given periods for a number of different professions. Let's have a look at it.

Annual Fatality Rates by Profession	Deaths per 100,000 full-time equivalents
Miners (2000-2010)	25
Commercial Fisherman (2000-2010)	124
Alaskan Bush Pilots (1990-2009)	287
U.S. military in Iraq (2003-2007)	335
Everest Sherpas (2000-2010)	1,332
Everest Sherpas (2004-2014)	4,053

This looks very clear, and they even produced a pretty diagram with big yellow circles to illustrate it visually. Sure enough, there seems to have been a shocking number of deaths among climbing Sherpas – a staggering 4,053 between 2004 and 2014 – which on the diagram looks a bit like Jupiter on a comparison of the planets. But hang on a minute, there have only been 255 deaths on Everest ever, since the very first expedition in 1921, and of those only 97 of them were Sherpas, so how come this table says there were 4,053 in just the 10-year period from 2004 to 2014? If you delve in a little more deeply, *Outside* tell us that 4,053 is a projected figure based on 'United States Bureau of Labor Statistics' formula for fatality rates per 100,000 full-time equivalents'. They don't explain how this calculation is made, but after a bit of digging around I found it in a PDF file on the US Bureau of Labor Statistics' website.[41] Here it is.

$(N \div EH) \times 200{,}000{,}000$, where

N = number of fatal injuries,

EH = total hours worked by all employees during the calendar year, and

$200{,}000{,}000$ = base for 100,000 equivalent full-time workers (working 40 hours per week, 50 weeks per year)

As you can see things are starting to get a little more complicated – in order to do the calculation, it's necessary to know the *total hours worked by all employees during the calendar year*. And this is where the second sore thumb sticks out and pokes me in the eye. As I've mentioned I'm no scientist, but once upon a time many years ago I did complete a degree in mathematics, and although I didn't exactly graduate with flying colours, I did learn enough to know that if you're going to extrapolate a large figure from a much smaller one – in this case deriving 4,053 projected Sherpa deaths in the period 2004 to 2014 from 30 actual ones, a 135-fold increase – you had better make sure the data you are using to perform the calculation is accurate, otherwise a very small error is going to become a very large error indeed.

Outside appear to be aware of this issue. They acknowledge that Sherpas don't clock in and out like workers in other service industries in the US, and that employers don't pay them by the hour. But they state that they 'consulted with guides, outfitters, and climbers to arrive at numbers we felt gave a fair picture of just how dangerous the job was'.[42] In other words, it's a guesstimate. They provide no data, just an assurance that they have the data and they believe it to be accurate.

Let's suppose for a minute that we have an aspiring research scientist with a hypothesis (that being a climbing Sherpa is more dangerous than fighting in a war), who has carried out some research they believe backs up this startling theory. Now they would like to have it published in a respectable journal and be taken seriously by the academic community. Here are some of the questions the journal's reviewers are likely to ask.

- Who were the guides, outfitters and climbers you talked to? Did you talk to any Sherpas as well?
- How did you calculate the number of hours a climbing Sherpa works in a calendar year? Does it include time the Sherpa spends at base camp, trekking in and using transport to get to and from the mountain? Does it include any time they may spend in Kathmandu preparing for the expedition, such as buying and packing equipment, and unpacking and drying tents afterwards? Does it include treks or expeditions to other mountains the Sherpa might do in a calendar year as part of their

employment, or are you only including time they spend on the most dangerous one, Everest, in your calculations?
- In your calculation of how many hours a US soldier works in a calendar year, are you including time they spend back in the barracks, carrying out drills, training, paperwork, packing and maintaining equipment, travelling between locations, etc. (and anything else a soldier may do outside actual fighting), or are you only including time they spend on the front line in a battle situation, the most dangerous part of their job, in your calculations?
- How do you define 'Everest Sherpas'? Do you mean just those who climb above base camp and have climbing permits for the summit, or do you include other mountaineering workers such as cooks and kitchen staff, porters and admin staff back in Kathmandu?
- How do you define 'US military in Iraq'? Do you mean just those who fight on the front line in a battle situation, or do you include officers with desk jobs, support staff such as engineers, doctors and other medical staff, or those working in IT, construction, logistics, firefighting, catering, etc.?
- Are your figures accurate, or are they only an estimate (bear in mind that small errors will be magnified significantly by your formula)?
- Do your figures include all Sherpas who have worked on Everest in the period 2004 to 2014, or are you using just a sample group from a smaller number of expedition teams? If it's just a sample how confident are you that the sample is representative? How did you determine the sample size required for the results to be significant? How

many Sherpa deaths occurred within the sample group (presumably it wasn't all 30 that occurred among Everest Sherpas within that period)?

Outside magazine have many questions to answer (and likely a lot of work to do) before their research can be considered trustworthy and be taken seriously by the scientific community. There are many assumptions and estimates that would wildly alter the figure for total hours worked by all employees during the calendar year. Many a bad scientist has been guilty of fudging their data to produce the outcome they desire, and it looks to me very much like *Outside* magazine has been guilty of precisely this.

Plenty of otherwise respectable publications seem to be happy to take *Outside* magazine's word for it and help them spread their agenda, and unfortunately it does appear to be an agenda. By far the most widely cited article that supports it is one called 'The Disposable Man' (a title that insults Sherpas and westerners in equal measure). One of its most frequently cited quotes is that there is 'no other service industry in the world that so frequently kills and maims its workers for the benefit of paying clients'.[43]

This alarming claim is not backed up by data in the article, but it is now apparent it's the same data used in their 18 April article that I have raised questions about above. In other words, data that is highly suspect. The danger with using unashamedly tendentious and misleading claims like this is that they defeat the purpose of making them in the first place, which is to improve lives for the Sherpa community. Moderate people suspect the article of bias and ignore it, while haters use it to hate even more. Truth is not served by either of these things.

Then of course there is the danger, now very real, that tourists will stop visiting Nepal. High-altitude mountaineers are the hardcore. They return to the country again and again, love its mountains, its people, and the bustle of Kathmandu. They have a lot of experience, and understand the risks and working conditions of Sherpas much better than the casual reader. They share many of the same risks and are not swayed by Everest hate. But the trekking industry that has developed from mountaineering is different; many of these people are first-time visitors to Nepal who understandably don't want to travel there if workers are going to be killed and maimed for their benefit, sent to war or shelled like soldiers on the front line.

So please, journalists, lovers of Nepal, whoever you are, let's have an end to this damaging nonsense. Everest is not a war zone. It can be dangerous, but it can also provide opportunities and fulfil dreams. Sherpas and clients alike climb it of their own free will, with some understanding of the risks they take. Look in the mirror and ask yourselves whether you are saying these things because you genuinely want to help Sherpas or simply to denigrate commercial Everest climbers and operators. If it's the former, and you really want to improve the lives of those in Nepal who work in the adventure travel industry, then please moderate the tone, stop producing and parroting cod science that incites hate and deliberately misleads, and start a dialogue with those of us who provide employment to Sherpas, have enjoyed many expeditions with them, and would like to improve their lives as much as you do.

And please let's not forget that mountaineering can be dangerous and 16 people did lose their lives. We owe it to their families to be dignified about their deaths and learn from the tragedy in constructive ways.

15
MY REVIEW OF
SHERPA – TROUBLE ON EVEREST

17 February 2016

I expect that not too many people have found themselves in a movie theatre watching a two-hour film about a real-life drama for which they have been an eyewitness. In December I had that experience for the first, and perhaps the only, time in my life.

Sherpa was released in a few select cinemas here in the UK just before Christmas, but it didn't get much coverage in the press. The day before I left for Ecuador I managed to catch a matinee screening at the Bertha DocHouse, a tiny arts cinema tucked away in the basement of the Curzon in Bloomsbury.

The film is a documentary focusing on the events of 18 April 2014, when a huge avalanche in the Khumbu Icefall on Everest killed 16 Sherpas and mountain workers. The tragedy was followed by a labour dispute that effectively closed the mountain for climbing a week later.

I was on my way into the Khumbu Icefall that morning, and around two hours away from the site of the accident. I witnessed the avalanche as it fell, and I witnessed many of the events which followed. I went to see this film with a certain amount of trepidation. A media frenzy followed the tragedy, during which western climbers like me were presented as heartless egotists who exploit Sherpas for our own gain, with little appreciation for the dangers they face on our behalf.

If you are a regular reader of my blog, you will know that the politics and economics of mountaineering in Nepal is a complex subject, and that dissecting this popular caricature of the modern Everest climber is a favourite hobby of mine. While I have an emotional attachment to the events and strong opinions about it, I'm going to try and make this a simple film review. Happily this has been made easier for me, because *Sherpa* is an excellent film that manages to achieve the difficult balance of being powerful and emotionally heart-rending, while remaining objective and factually accurate.

I believe the film does great credit to Sherpas by not simply presenting them as oppressed heroes (as they are in the popular media caricature), but by steering an enlightened path through the politics, culture and economics of the mountaineering industry that forms such an important part of their lives.

The characters

The leading character in the story is Phurba Tashi Sherpa, sirdar of the expedition operator Himex. He is one of the best known of all Sherpas. He holds the record for the greatest number of ascents of Everest (21, held jointly with Apa Sherpa) and was one of my ten great Sherpa mountaineers of a previous article.

The most important supporting character is Phurba Tashi's boss Russell Brice, owner of Himex: a western operator at the luxury end of the market, and one of the pioneers of commercial mountaineering on Everest.

Perhaps the most inspired piece of casting is that of the narrator, Ed Douglas. A journalist and mountaineering historian, we hear his voice throughout the film, providing background to the drama and helping to describe the events as they unfold. As a journalist he is not afraid to provide a critical eye where necessary; as a historian his knowledge and love of Nepal and mountaineering shine through, providing a balance required by the complexity of the story. We even get to see him from time to time, huddled inside his down jacket at base camp, like a storyteller recounting his tale beside the campfire.

Background

The film begins in Khumjung, the Sherpa village near Namche Bazaar which is Phurba Tashi's home. The Everest season is about to start and his family don't want him to go. His wife lost her brother in a climbing accident the previous year and she can't believe Phurba still wishes to climb.

As footage of mountains and Buddhist stupas pan across the screen we hear Phurba's voice presenting the other side. He says he likes his job, and he talks about how important it is for him to earn money. He describes how Everest work benefits everyone in the Sherpa community, including cooks, porters and teahouse owners.

Ed Douglas then provides some historical background. He tells us how Sherpas knew nothing about mountaineering in the early days; they just happened to be strong at high altitude, and were employed by European climbers exploring the Himalayas.

Jamling Tenzing, son of the great Tenzing Norgay, provides a hybrid perspective. He is an ethnic Sherpa who has climbed Everest, but he received a western education and lives in the United States. He talks about how everybody in the west assumes that all Sherpas climb Everest and have no idea that Sherpas are an ethnic race of people.

He contrasts the difference in perspective between Sherpas and westerners. For Sherpas Chomolungma (Everest) is holy, but to most westerners it is just an extreme physical challenge.

'Not all westerners understand this,' he says, 'but some do.'

Russell Brice is introduced. Phurba Tashi explains how he wouldn't have his job were it not for Russell and neither would any of the 25 Sherpas working for him, all of whom he hired.

We are given a smaller taste of the frequently overlooked commercial clients' perspective. As footage is shown of Sherpas working hard at base camp, setting up a plasma-screen telly, bookshelves and comfy lounge seats, some of Russell's clients are interviewed and talk about their reasons for wanting to climb Everest.

The Khumbu Icefall

If *Sherpa* were a horror movie, the Khumbu Icefall would be the chainsaw-wielding psychopath lurking in the background, never understood but always feared.

As we watch time-lapse footage of the Khumbu Icefall moving down from the Western Cwm like a river of ice, Ed Douglas explains how the icefall is constantly moving, with crevasses opening up and towers of ice toppling over. The route through it requires constant maintenance; while the dangers can be lessened, there is no way of avoiding the icefall.

'Is it worth the risk?' he says directly to camera.

'On no other mountain in the world would anyone think about going through a place like the Khumbu Icefall,' Russell Brice says, 'but on Everest it's normal. Every time my Sherpas go up there I feel like I'm sending them into a war zone.'

He explains that while his clients go off to acclimatise on Lobuje East and will pass through the icefall only twice, some of his Sherpas will be going through it 20 to 30 times.

Sherpa tension

The Khumbu Icefall is not the only malevolent force running through this story. It is also a story of conflict involving workers, their bosses, their clients and government. The next part of the film focuses on the Sherpa dissatisfaction bubbling beneath the surface.

Sumit Joshi of the Nepali expedition operator Himalayan Ascent explains how 80 per cent of Sherpas are now educated – a recent development. Dawa Steven Sherpa of the Nepali operator Asian Trekking talks about the Facebook generation, and how younger Sherpas are feeling resentful after seeing western clients taking the glory for climbing Everest.

We see footage of a fight that occurred between Sherpas and western climbers at Camp 2 on Everest in 2013, after the Italian mountaineer Simone Moro called one of the Sherpa rope-fixing team a 'motherfucker'. We see Sherpas throwing rocks at a tent, Moro being given a slap, and we hear the voice of Swiss climber Ueli Steck describing how he thought they were going to be killed.

Russell Brice explains how the younger generation of Sherpas are less deferential, and sometimes that concerns him.

At this point in the film, there is no mention of the political background, or how it contributes to the resentment.

The 18 April avalanche

We come to the moment when all this fuel is ignited.

We see head-camera footage of a climber (presumably a Sherpa) walking along a snow bridge and becoming engulfed in darkness. Russell Brice is shown with his radio asking Phil Crampton, another expedition operator, if his Sherpas are OK.

Next we see Russell arguing with Pasang Tenzing Sherpa and the 'mountain guides'. We are not told who the mountain guides are, but I presume they are members of the Nepal National Mountain Guide Association (NNMGA). Around 30 Nepalis are UIAGM-qualified mountain guides. I understand that only about four of these (including Pasang Tenzing) work on Everest. The remainder, it seemed from the film, had been flown into base camp that morning by helicopter.

Russell wants to send two doctors up to the accident site by helicopter, but the mountain guides believe they should be flown up first. Russell speaks to a western voice in the icefall who says they would like the doctors to be sent up first (this would make sense – I can confirm there were plenty of uninjured and experienced Sherpas up in the icefall who were able to help with a rescue).

We see dramatic footage of the rescue, with bodies brought down by helicopters on long lines. The casualties come first, followed by the dead.

The protests

After my expedition was cancelled in 2014, I remember

returning to Kathmandu and sitting in cafés and bars in a state of bewilderment, unable to make sense of what had happened.

The next part of the film brought a part of that back to me. In some ways it was enlightening. The protests were mostly conducted in Nepali, and though we were witnesses at the time, we could only guess at what was happening. By providing English subtitles the film provided some answers for me – but it also raised more questions.

In some ways, viewers who watch *Sherpa* without the background and deeper understanding that I have might get a taste of this too. The film is enlightening, but the sheer complexity is also bewildering.

We see the protestors at work: Pasang Bhote with his colourful purple beanie, Pasang Tenzing in his distinctive camouflage baseball cap, and Sumit Joshi, who with his fluent command of English is the main spokesman when westerners are being addressed. This is consistent with who I perceived to be the main leaders of the protest in my position as an eyewitness.

We see how government action helped to fuel the protest – when they offered derisory compensation to the victims' families – and we see how government *in*action failed to prevent a strike, when officials flew into base camp and provided no assurances.

We see the utter confusion of the Himex clients as they ask their western guides to explain what is happening. The guides have no idea either. The anger of some of them is illustrated by one client who rants into the camera, likening the protestors to terrorists (I should point out that while I shared some of his frustration, his interpretation of events lies at the extreme end of the spectrum).

The helplessness of operators, and the unwillingness of most Sherpas to get involved in the dispute, is beautifully illustrated by a single meeting between Russell and his Sherpas. Russell asks if they want to continue with the expedition; none of them, not even Phurba Tashi, is willing to offer an opinion. Russell interprets their silence in the only way he can. He cancels the expedition, Phurba nods and the meeting ends.

Perhaps the most mind-boggling factor of all is whether the strike was enforced by the threat of violence. To this day I am yet to meet a single person who is willing to admit that they were physically threatened. But one thing I know for sure: base camp was rife with rumours of the threat of violence. Does this in itself constitute a threat? I have no idea.

Anyone watching *Sherpa* will be left convinced that these threats were completely fabricated, and they will conclude this from two successive sequences.

At the meeting with his Sherpas, Russell asks if they have been threatened. There is silence, but Phurba eventually admits that he himself has not been threatened (unlike most teams, Russell's Sherpas returned to Khumjung immediately after the avalanche to see their families, and were not at base camp during the protests).

In the very next sequence, we see Russell explaining to his clients that he is reluctantly having to cancel their expedition because Phurba and his Sherpas have been threatened with violence.

This was a mistake on Russell's part. I'm none the wiser about whether expeditions had to be cancelled because of the threat of violence. He wasn't in an easy position and I'm sure he tried hard to keep climbing, but one thing I know for certain is that as a commercial client I prefer my operator to be honest with me.

The future

'My father said he climbed Everest so that we wouldn't have to,' says Norbu Tenzing, oldest son of Tenzing Norgay, in the closing sequences.

This sentiment was echoed by the Sherpas in our team whom I spoke to after my own ascent of Everest in 2012. None of them wanted their children to follow in their footsteps, and they hoped that by providing them with a good education they would be able to take up other careers.

'I hope there will now be a calm about Everest, instead of all the madness,' we hear Ed Douglas say.

I felt myself nodding in agreement when I heard this, but I'm not hopeful of it happening.

The conclusion of the film is probably its weakest part. In trying to tie up some of the loose ends I believe it lets viewers down a little. There are no easy answers to the Everest conundrum; in many ways the situation has become even worse.

The makers of the film could not have predicted the earthquake the following year that killed around 9,000 people, or the political dispute and border blockade that only came to an end earlier this month and has had an even more devastating effect on Nepal. The earthquake is mentioned in a single sentence of text appearing on screen. Another sentence asserts that 'the government eventually agreed to all Sherpa demands'.

Sadly it didn't. Very few of them were ever met and the government has since talked of backtracking on those that were.

At the end of the film, Phurba Tashi says that he will not climb again – but, sadly for Phurba, one of the greats among Sherpas and a true hero, there has been no happy ending. The earthquake destroyed his home. With no insurance he

MY REVIEW OF SHERPA – TROUBLE ON EVEREST

will have to work again to rebuild it.[44]

Everest is just a small part of the bigger tragedy that is today's Nepal. The wider political context is not discussed in the film, understandably.

A culture of strikes and corruption has dogged the country for many years. Following the earthquake, a politically motivated blockade on the India-Nepal border deprived ordinary Nepalis of essential supplies and fuelled a damaging black-market economy. The majority of the $4 billion pledged in international donations after the earthquake remains unspent. Many people have died in temporary accommodation over the winter.

This film can only touch upon a small part of that, but it does so with skill and sensitivity. It deserves to be watched more widely, and I extend my thanks to its makers.

Harrowing scenes at Everest base camp as a helicopter airlifts a victim of the avalanche on a long line.

16
EVEREST'S DEADLIEST DAY – DEBATING EVEREST'S FUTURE

15 October 2014

'Everest's Deadliest Day' was the title of a debate at the Royal Geographical Society in London last week. The event was billed as an expert panel of the world's top mountaineers discussing April's avalanche in the Khumbu Icefall that killed 16 climbing Sherpas, and what it meant for the future of Himalayan climbing and the economy of Nepal.

Having seen the avalanche happen as I walked through base camp that morning on my own way into the icefall, and witnessed many of the events that followed, it was a debate I didn't want to miss. The organisers had put together an interesting group of people. Without wishing to malign the other panellists, Doug Scott was the only one who could reasonably describe himself as one of the 'world's top mountaineers'. This was actually a good thing. All too often when a controversial story emerges about Everest, the media rushes to get the opinion of an elite climber, but Everest's future has many stakeholders whose views are equally valid, and this debate included a broader cross section.

As the first Briton to climb Everest (in 1975) and one of the country's greatest ever mountaineers, Doug Scott represented the alpinists and advocates of a purer style of climbing on Everest, but as founder of the charity Community Action Nepal he also has a broader understanding of what this might mean for Nepal. Rebecca Stephens brought a similar charity perspective as chair of Sir Edmund Hillary's Himalayan Trust UK. She was also the first British woman to climb Everest, in 1993. Journalist and mountaineering historian Ed Douglas provided the media perspective, but it was the other two panellists whose views I was most interested in hearing. Simon Lowe is managing director of the British expedition operator Jagged Globe, who lost a climbing Sherpa in the tragedy; Dawa Steven Sherpa is managing director of Asian Trekking, the biggest Nepali operator, and an ethnic Sherpa. It seems we are not yet ready to ask the opinion of two other important stakeholders, the commercial clients and the climbing Sherpas, but one step at a time. I live in hope this will happen one day, and Simon and Dawa's participation represents a big step forward in the debate.

The other member of the panel was its chair, Ben Ayers: Nepal country director for dZi Foundation, the event organisers. Pronounced *zee*, the dzi is a stone some Nepalis wear as a necklace to bestow health and protection. The dZi Foundation provides support for rural villages in Nepal in the form of community development projects. This debate was intended to raise both funds and their profile, and in this respect it was effective in my case – I hadn't heard of them before and was interested to read about some of the work they do. Ben has lived and worked in Nepal for 15 years, so had lots of interesting insider knowledge about the country to bring to the debate, though for the most part he kept out of it and played devil's advocate with a series of leading (and sometimes loaded) questions.

He started by asking each member of the panel where they were the moment they heard about the tragedy. Only one of them, Dawa, was at base camp, although Ed had been in Kathmandu in a meeting with the Himalayan chronicler Elizabeth Hawley, and Simon arguably found himself equally close to the action. He was at home in Sheffield, but had to take a call in the middle of the night to learn that one of his climbing Sherpas had been killed and several others injured. He immediately flew to Nepal to meet their families (though declined an invitation from his expedition leader to take a helicopter to base camp and experience altitude sickness).

Ben asked Doug to describe his ascent of Everest in 1975. It was a siege-style expedition, involving teams of support climbers carrying loads of equipment up to a series of camps as they gradually worked their way up to a position from which they could make a summit attempt. But otherwise, it had virtually nothing else in common with today's commercial expeditions. They were the only team on the mountain – in accordance with the permit rules in those days – and made the first ascent of the south-west face, a route that has received only a handful of ascents since. It took place in the autumn season, and there were no fixed ropes on summit day for the climbers to slide up with jumars, as commercial climbers do. Doug Scott and Dougal Haston arrived on the summit late in the afternoon and had to bivouac by the south summit on the way down. Only three other climbers (Pete Boardman, Pertemba Sherpa and probably Mick Burke, who went missing) reached the top after them; the rest of the team were content to play support roles.

'And how should Everest be climbed these days?' Ben asked.

'The same way,' Doug replied.

This was the first debating point, and Dawa responded by saying that today Everest is more than just a mountain to be climbed. It provides jobs and livelihoods for the whole community, from climbing Sherpas to kitchen staff, porters and teahouse owners. It is a means for Sherpas to provide for their families, send their children to school and give them the opportunity for a better quality of life. He pointed out that Everest could still be climbed in the manner Doug described on any one of Everest's 18 other routes, or by climbing in the autumn season when nobody else was there. Ed backed this up by saying Everest was Nepal's 'calling card' for the whole of its travel industry. Nepal needs Everest expeditions. Publicity for Everest impacts tourism elsewhere in the country.

Ben then showed a short video clip of the celebrated climbers Melissa Arnot and Simone Moro talking about a party at base camp, followed by footage of some sort of rave inside a large dome tent. He showed Ralf Dujmovits's much-publicised photo of a queue of climbers on the Lhotse Face, and another of a traffic jam on the Hillary Step.

'Doug, did they have parties like that at base camp in your day?' Ben said. There were a few chuckles in the audience.

Again it was Dawa who responded. 'These photos are not representative,' he said. 'In 2012, when those pictures were taken, we were late fixing ropes that season. There was rockfall on the Lhotse Face early in the season and a Sherpa was injured. This caused some teams to pull out of the rope-fixing duties that are usually shared. We missed two weather windows for rope fixing, and that year there were only two very short windows for summiting. Normally at any one moment there will be climbers at base camp, and climbers spread out at other camps. That year everybody was on the mountain at the same time. What you see in that photo is everyone who was on the mountain. This was an exceptional case.'

But Ben wasn't finished. He showed a short clip of an interview with Norbu Tenzing, son of the great Tenzing Norgay. Norbu talked about how Sherpas have always been treated as second-class citizens by the westerners who came to climb Everest.

'I disagree with Norbu,' Ed said. 'Sherpas aren't victims. They are extremely resourceful. I find this attitude a bit patronising, and it doesn't reflect how things are.' Dawa nodded his agreement.

Perhaps inevitably Ben also showed footage of the brawl between Sherpas and climbers at Camp 2 last year and asked the panel for their thoughts.

Simon responded by providing the view from Yorkshire. 'If anyone walks into a pub in Sheffield and calls someone the word Simone used, they are likely to start a fight, and they might get their mates to join in.'

Dawa was a little more diplomatic. 'What those Sherpas did was wrong, but you have to understand that it's a big deal for those guys out in front doing the rope fixing. It's a great honour and a big day in their lives. To have people climbing alongside them without fixed ropes and speaking to them so disrespectfully was hurtful, and emotions were running high.'

I personally felt that Ben was taking his devil's-advocate role a little too far by pitching the debate at the level of tabloid-style headlines. I didn't believe for a minute that he agreed with some of the questions he was putting to the panel to elicit a response. At one point he asked if they thought climbing Everest was *ethical*. None of them bothered to answer this question directly, but they had already answered it indirectly many times over by describing the importance of Everest expeditions to Sherpas and Nepal in general. He even slipped in a slide containing *Outside* magazine's frequently parroted assertion that being a climbing Sherpa is more dangerous than being a soldier in Iraq, and quickly moved on without giving the panel an opportunity to question the assertion (which I have previously debunked). The audience were a little more educated than this, IMHO, and even if any of us believed all the stories we read in the media, we were soon enlightened by the panel.

Thankfully the debate did become more mature, and there was an opportunity to discuss the finer detail about how commercial mountaineering on Everest should be managed in the future. While commercial clients like myself have taken a battering in the media and online discussion forums, the expedition operators have had a harder time of it, and have often been portrayed as villains who mistreat the Sherpas working for them. With Simon and Dawa on the panel we were able to find out what operators do for the families of their employees when tragedy occurs.

Dawa gave us some figures about the insurance cover that is provided for death, helicopter evacuation and medical fees. The death insurance has been widely publicised because it was one of the demands Sherpa protestors made to the Nepali government during the industrial dispute that followed the avalanche. There was some discussion between Dawa and Simon about the exact figure, but my understanding is that it was US$10,000 at the time, and has since been increased to $15,000. This is the maximum amount: in other words, Nepali insurers do not insure for more than this. Dawa said that it's not possible for operators to insure their climbing Sherpas with foreign insurance companies. It's debatable whether this is enough given that Everest climbing Sherpas often have to support extended families. However, even in the west, life insurance generally only covers immediate family long enough for them to find an alternative source of income (typically four times annual salary).

'It's never enough,' Dawa said when Ben put the question to him.

It then becomes the responsibility of operators to ensure that families are looked after, and this is where there can be great disparity. Simon explained that he met the family of Pasang Karma, the Sherpa employed by Jagged Globe who died in the avalanche, and they have made a commitment to support them for an extended period. While they would like to be able to do this for any employee, he admitted that it would have been very difficult to make such a commitment had five Sherpas died in the tragedy – as happened with the US operator Alpine Ascents – and that it may well have bankrupted them. In the case of a major tragedy like this, however, the international community rallies round with donations, as I have highlighted previously.

Ed stepped into the discussion by explaining that, where Sherpa welfare is concerned, often it is the Nepali operators who are at fault. They hire staff who are less experienced, pay them a fraction of what the western operators pay, and fail to insure them adequately. Surprisingly, Dawa agreed (although Ed did say that Asian Trekking were an exception). Dawa said there was no regulation, that it was possible for any Nepali to take money from a client, register as a trekking agency, and organise an expedition to climb Everest. Many people had done this, and operated for just a single season. If there were any problems they could simply dissolve the company and register a new one under a different name. Simon explained that often the bigger operators picked up the pieces if climbers who had chosen to climb with one of these rogue agencies needed to be rescued.

The panel talked about whether steps should be taken to limit the numbers of people who climb Everest. Unsurprisingly, Doug was the most passionate advocate, but even he was not against all forms of commercial mountaineering on Everest.

'Everyone who climbs Everest should be able to demonstrate they have climbed at least two 7,000m peaks,' he said. 'This will spread the numbers around, get climbers onto other mountains and benefit people in other parts of Nepal.'

'This might be a good idea in principle,' Ed said, 'but it's not realistic to expect it will happen, as there is no will from government to limit numbers.'

Ben asked the panel what they thought about stunts, bizarre records and the numbers of people using Everest as a stepping stone for other careers, such as sponsored adventurer or public speaker.

'Can I ask you, Rebecca, as someone who received a lot of publicity for being the first?' he said.

'When I first came back from Everest the question I was asked most (apart from "what's next?", which was even more annoying) was whether Everest had changed me,' Rebecca said. 'I didn't think it had changed me. I had no money and I needed a job, and I still needed both when I came back. But in hindsight, I have to say that Everest changed my life completely, and I can't in conscience criticise anyone else for wanting to be the first.'

Rebecca is an exception in that she has been able to make a career from it. I was never going to be able to quit my day job after becoming the 318th Briton to climb Everest, and the same is true for most people who climb it, though it will always be a big event in our lives. Dawa appeared to agree.

'It depends what the first is. On my team this year we had someone who was aiming to be the first black South

African woman to climb Everest. She was strong and motivated. I don't see there is anything wrong with anyone wanting to push themselves and achieve something like that. If she succeeds she will be inspirational to others. Then there was another time when I had two clients who came and said "We want a record – can we be the first couple to climb Everest?" That was bizarre, and I don't get that.'

Ben concluded the discussion by asking the panel what they thought people in the room could do to improve the situation on Everest. Doug replied that anyone who wanted to climb it had a responsibility to look after the welfare of staff who worked for them. This included researching the credentials of any agency they used to ensure they paid their staff a fair wage and insured them adequately. Rebecca reminded us that we can still donate to the Himalayan Trust. Simon added that potential climbers needed to educate themselves beforehand. They needed to understand that climbing Everest is not easy. He said that journalists also had a responsibility to report accurately, and that they were partly to blame for this popular misconception.

Media sensationalism was one of many issues that was only briefly discussed during the evening. Ed Douglas is perhaps unique in being a journalist writing for a mainstream publication (*The Guardian*) who is an expert on Nepal and commercial mountaineering on Everest, and writes about it objectively without pursuing a particular agenda. It would have been unfair for him to take the rap for the faults of others in his profession. On one of the few occasions the subject arose, he said it was ridiculous that climbers could blog about a rumour they heard in base camp and it would be reported as fact in the media the following day.

Despite my frustration at the level of debate posed by some of the questions at the beginning, I enjoyed the evening. I left with the feeling that despite the different backgrounds of the panellists, they were largely in agreement that commercial mountaineering on Everest is not only inevitable, but a good thing for Nepal. The question is not *whether* it is ethical, but how to manage it in a way that provides the most benefit for the communities who rely on it – both in Nepal and outside.

Ben said that the dZi Foundation intended to make the Everest debate an annual event, and asked the audience to think of ideas for the next one. This isn't difficult, as there were many issues either only touched upon briefly or not covered at all. I've mentioned media sensationalism; pollution and the environment is another popular topic that didn't get much time here, although it does frequently in the media. Climbing ethics were never discussed: should limitations be placed on the level of support provided to commercial clients? What if anything did the panel think was likely to change after the tragedy? We didn't talk much about risk. We all know that climbing Everest is no picnic, but just how dangerous is it and what can be done to make it safer? And then there is the politics. I would love to have known what the panel thought of the Sherpa strike that followed the avalanche, and the many demands they made to government. Were climbers and operators their target, or were we just caught in the crossfire of a dispute with government? Nepal's Ministry of Tourism got off lightly, although Ed did briefly allude to some of their failings. He mentioned that permit fees were primarily just a revenue generator for government, rather than being invested in regulation and services on the mountain. He could have gone further and talked about the widespread corruption (there was a delegation from the Nepalese embassy present, although they left during the interval). Some of these questions were discussed on the Twitter hashtag *#dzieverest* after the event, and I'm sure after the 2015 season the debate will have moved on even more.

The Everest base camp summit meeting, 2014.

PART THREE

TRIUMPH

17
ON SUMMIT CERTIFICATES, LIAISON OFFICERS AND FUNNY MOUNTAINEERING RULES

20 July 2016

In a surprise announcement, *The Himalayan Times* has reported that Sherpas who climbed Everest this year will not be receiving summit certificates.[45] This follows reports that a pair of Indian police officers (of all people) did receive summit certificates in exchange for Photoshopping a pair of summit photos.[46]

So what on earth is going on? Once again, here at the *Footsteps on the Mountain* blog, I try to shed some light on the bizarre workings of Nepal's Ministry of Tourism.

But first some history. Recognition for their help in getting westerners up high mountains has been an important part of Sherpa culture for the best part of 100 years.

As more mountaineering expeditions used Darjeeling as their base for exploring the Himalayas, and recruited porters to transport their many tons of equipment over high passes, it became important for Sherpas who had worked on previous expeditions to have references from their employers.

The system was formalised with the foundation of the Himalayan Club in 1928. They established a more organised system of recruiting porters, which included a passbook for each mountain worker, listing their name, village and contact details, and a list of the previous expeditions they had worked on. At the end of each expedition, their employers would add a line to the book confirming each Sherpa's employment. It was the responsibility of the Sherpa to look after this book and produce it at the recruitment ground when a new expedition arrived looking for staff.

Remnants of this system are still in place. I often ask Sherpas I climb with about the other mountains they have climbed, and all of them happily reel off the exact tally of their 8,000m peak summits. This is because it's more than just a status symbol: their 8,000m summits can directly affect their ability to find work. Formal recognition in the form of a summit certificate is therefore very important.

So why did Nepal's Ministry of Tourism refuse to issue Sherpas their summit certificates this year?

According to *The Himalayan Times*, the answer lies in one of the Rule 32s of the Mountaineering Expedition Regulation, a set of rules governing the behaviour of foreign mountaineering expeditions (and which contains two Rule 32s but no Rule 33). In the article, Laxman Sharma of the Ministry of Tourism's Mountaineering Section, explains the regulation. He says that the regulation states the government should provide a certificate to 'members of the successful expedition' but not to its Sherpas.

But here's what the regulation actually says:

32. Certificate to be Provided: The Ministry shall provide a certificate of mountaineering expedition to the mountaineering expedition team and the member of such team for successful mountaineering expedition in the

FUNNY MOUNTAINEERING RULES

format as prescribed in schedule 13.[47]

If you can read beyond the legal-style language, you can see that it doesn't say anything about 'but not to Sherpas'. If we're going to cite this rule as a basis for issuing certificates, it doesn't say anything about reaching the summit either. Taken literally, as long as the expedition is successful, every member of the team should get a certificate.

So what on earth is Mr Sharma talking about? He goes on to say that the regulation only applies to those who have obtained a climbing permit by paying a royalty to the government (i.e. a permit fee). Sherpas are therefore not considered members of the team. But I've been through the regulation several times now, and although it talks about team 'member' in several places, it makes no definition about what a team member is. Nowhere does it exclude Sherpas from this definition.

Moreover, the document was written in 2002 and Sherpas have always been issued with summit certificates until now. There are several other rules mentioned in the document that are routinely ignored, including by the Ministry of Tourism itself.

For example, Rule 8 states that 'His Majesty's Government shall designate a liaison officer' to accompany the expedition ('His Majesty' being the king, who was deposed in 2008 when the monarchy was abolished and Nepal became a republic). The regulation lists a number of functions and duties of the liaison officer, one of which is 'to stay in the base camp during the mountaineering expedition program'.[48]

But I've been on several mountaineering expeditions in Nepal, and I've never once had a Nepalese liaison officer stay with me in base camp. In fact, I've never even met any of my liaison officers. This is because expedition liaison officers rarely show up for work, and this fact is widely known. Barely a week before this article, Rajan Pokhrel of *The Himalayan Times* (who deserves a certificate of his own for breaking news about Nepal's tourism industry) reported that of 33 liaison officers assigned to mountaineering expeditions on Everest this year, only 17 of them even made it to base camp.[49]

He goes on to list the 16 expedition teams who never saw their liaison officer (but paid their wages). If only he had named and shamed the 16 officials who bunked off work as well, then the story would be complete. Another of the things the expedition liaison officer is supposed to do is to carry out or initiate 'the necessary work relating to environmental cleanness and garbage management'. But if he or she doesn't show up for work then expedition teams are able to ignore these responsibilities.

There are some other funny rules in the mountaineering regulations that are destined to be broken. Rule 21 states that expedition teams should provide their staff with an opportunity to climb to the summit if they accompany the team as far as the last camp. But this is a mountaineering decision – one that has to be taken at the time, depending on the circumstances. It's not something that should be governed by red tape. Climbing Sherpas are employed first and foremost to help the team, and the needs of the team must come before any personal ambition to reach the summit.

Rule 7 states that teams are permitted to import two satellite phones, twelve walkie-talkies and two wirelesses into the country for the purposes of communicating between base camp, Kathmandu and the nearest police station, as long as they take them back out again. These regulations were written in 2002, a few years after the invention of the internet, but in an era when the Ministry of Tourism believed that people were still using wireless as a means of communicating with Kathmandu. Why not runners bearing coded messages? With 3G now available most of the way up to base camp, firing off an email with a smartphone or laptop is a bit more likely.

But first, they have to obey Rule 24, which states that the team must provide all news relating to the expedition to His Majesty's Government via their liaison officer. Which, of course, is a bit difficult if the liaison officer is nowhere to be seen. Another regulation that I wasn't aware of is Rule 31 Paragraph 4, which says that if any team member publishes a book relating to their expedition, they have to send two copies to the Ministry. Does this mean I'm supposed to send two copies of *Seven Steps from Snowdon to Everest*? They have to be joking.

But if I've convinced you that Nepal's Mountaineering Expedition Regulation is farcical, it seems that Mr Sharma of the Ministry of Tourism already knows this. According to the article, they are already amending the regulation, and Sherpas will be entitled to summit certificates in the future. If this is the case, then why not just give them the certificates they deserve, instead of adhering to rules that are flagrantly ignored in so many other ways?

Two years ago I was at Everest Base Camp when a Sherpa strike caused all expeditions on the mountain to be cancelled. The strike was ostensibly about an avalanche, but as time went on it became clear that it was actually a dispute between Sherpas and government about how the money from foreign mountaineering expeditions is spent. Climbers like me were caught in the crossfire.

Also, this month a team of climbers were barred from climbing a peak in Upper Mustang by locals who claimed their presence was a bad omen if they passed through land that was being cultivated. The climbers had paid their permit fee and believed they had permission to climb. But the locals weren't aware of this, and it's doubtful if any of the money found its way to them.[50]

In the short term the losers were the climbers, who had to go home with their peak unclimbed. But if the Ministry of Tourism continues to ignore the wishes of those who carry out the work or own the land, and tourists continue to lose out like I did in 2014, then all of Nepal's tourist industry will suffer in the long run.

This is a very simple reason why Sherpas should be given their certificates, to put alongside the even simpler ones that it costs nothing and it's the right thing to do.

18
ARE WESTERN OPERATORS RIGHT TO COMPLAIN ABOUT CHEAP NEPALI OPERATORS ON EVEREST?

4 May 2016

Last week *The Himalayan Times* reported how the rise of cheap Nepali operators who employ inexperienced Sherpas are increasing their market share of commercial Everest expeditions and making the mountain more dangerous.[51]

This is not a new story, but it has passed under the radar of western media, who prefer to focus on western operators and inexperienced western climbers, rather than Nepali operators and inexperienced Sherpas.

It was good to see the issue raised in *The Himalayan Times*, and I hope it gets taken up by western media. The article, written by Kathmandu-based journalist Ammu Kannampilly, provided a balanced picture, much better than most articles about Everest you will find published in the west, which tend to be simplistic and one-sided.

There are two sides to this issue, and I will do my best to outline both as I provide the commercial client's perspective.

Until recently, commercial Everest expeditions were run almost exclusively by western operators, who would often subcontract to Nepali trekking operators to provide their logistics to and from the mountain and at base camp. The western operators, however, provided all of the services higher up the mountain. These included qualified western guides and teams of experienced climbing Sherpas, whom they often employed directly.

The reasons for this are fairly clear. It was the western operators who were able to get the clients. They speak much better English (or French, German, Spanish, Italian, Russian, etc.), and are better at meeting their clients' expectations. Crucially they were also able to build up a word-of-mouth reputation. Western climbers felt more comfortable booking one of their own and climbing with western guides. Booking a Nepali operator felt like a risk. Clients didn't know any reliable ones, and had no idea where to start looking.

This situation has changed completely in the last three or four years, and the western operators have failed to adapt to changing times – including a big change in client perceptions.

For a number of reasons Nepali operators have become more adept at finding clients. They are better educated now, more westernised, and speak much better English. They have websites and Facebook friendships to link them with potential clients worldwide. Some are Sherpas who worked for western operators, formed friendships with western clients and, for want of a better word, poached them from their ex-employers.

There are also many Indian and Chinese clients climbing Everest now. They are more inclined to hire Nepali operators, and this has enabled the local operators to expand their business on Everest. Some climbers return to Everest after unsuccessful expeditions; they become more familiar with the Nepali operators they climb alongside, and are more inclined to trust them.

So that's one reason the Nepali operators are taking over on Everest: trust. The other main reason is a more controversial and emotive one: price.

There are various reasons why Nepali operators are able to offer cheaper prices for Everest expeditions. It may seem obvious, but the cost of living is much lower in Nepal. This includes the cost of an Everest climbing permit (which is also cheaper for a Nepali), but it also includes basic living expenses such as food, taxes, hospital fees, rent, property prices, school fees, etc. Western operators have to pay their western staff western wages to enable them to live a reasonable lifestyle in the west. This doesn't just mean the western guides that some of them provide for their clients on Everest; it also means all their office staff back home, and an income for themselves. They have to pay for flights, visa fees, hotel accommodation in Kathmandu, and somebody to feed the cat while they're away (OK, that last one was a bit silly, but you get the idea).

Nepali operators are also better at negotiating cheaper prices in Nepal. A white face with a wad of notes at a market in Kathmandu is going to get charged a lot more than a Nepali speaking the local language. The same applies to negotiating porter fees and almost every other product and service that needs to be purchased in Nepal. This expense isn't removed if the western operator subcontracts their logistics to a Nepali operator; the local operator knows their value to the western operator, and prices their services accordingly.

More controversially – and this was the main thrust of the article in *The Himalayan Times* – many Nepali operators (though not all) have a very different business ethic to western operators. They also have different attitudes to safety.

For the reasons I describe above, most western operators

pay their climbing Sherpas a lower wage than they pay their western guides, but they still pay them a good wage by Nepali standards. The most commonly cited figure is US$5,000 for a two-month Everest season compared to the $700 annual income for the average Nepali (the second figure is based on the World Bank's data for GNI per capita, which was $730 in 2014).[52] Some Nepali operators, on the other hand, pay their staff much less. Again, this figure is unverified, but I've heard $500 quoted for a full Everest season.

The article in *The Himalayan Times* quotes the owner of one of the largest Nepali operators. He excuses the huge disparity in wages by claiming that his Sherpas are not expected to do the same job as those Sherpas who work for western operators. He explains that he is offering young Sherpas a chance to learn. There is no safety issue because they will be carrying loads rather than guiding clients, and there is no need for him to provide technical training because they will be learning on the job from other Sherpas. Culturally this attitude may seem reasonable for a Nepali – and I would be happy for any Nepali reading this to correct me – but it will set alarm bells ringing among western operators.

They may only be carrying loads (and not guiding clients), but they are carrying loads through some of the most dangerous terrain on earth. The Khumbu Icefall requires a degree of technical skill that a Sherpa new to Everest may not have. There may be ladders, but a level of proficiency is needed when walking up steep ice in crampons and clipping into and out of fixed ropes. It needs to be done quickly and efficiently, and it requires confidence.

There is also the question of altitude. Due to their physiology, Sherpas perform much better at high altitude than westerners when fully acclimatised. However, contrary to popular belief, they are not naturals above 5,000m, and are just as susceptible to altitude sickness as everyone else. Wisdom at high altitude comes only with experience. This should not be learned for the first time in the Khumbu Icefall when you feel under pressure to do a good job for your employer.

Not only do western operators employ more experienced Sherpas and pay them better, but they have a much better pedigree when things go wrong. This is something that rarely gets written about. For reasons I don't fully understand, heroic rescues with a happy ending are a lot less appealing to media than disasters where somebody dies.

When things go wrong on Everest, experienced western operators fight tooth and nail to bring climbers down safely – a dead client is bad for business. Although this should apply equally to Nepali operators, many have not yet grasped this, and all too often the unnecessary deaths are climbers who have chosen the cheaper operators.

Cynics will say that operators are only acting in their own interests, but this is not the case. I have yet to meet a guide with such a casual regard to human life, and western operators frequently work together to help each other. Often the person best placed to help is on another team. With a quick radio call, a guide whose client is strong will go to help a competitor's client if they are struggling and need help. They frequently lend each other oxygen bottles. And if a climber is severely ill it can take resources beyond the capacity of a single team; some of the most heroic rescues take dozens of Sherpas and guides from multiple teams who happen to be in a position to assist. These rescues are common enough, but you rarely hear about them.

The larger western operators don't just help out each other – they often look after everyone on the mountain. Frequently, however, budget operators and independent climbers look to the larger operators to help them when things go wrong. I wrote about such an incident in my diary *Thieves, Liars and Mountaineers* when I was climbing Gasherbrum II in Pakistan in 2009. We were the only team with experienced climbing Sherpas. Late one evening a climber in need began signalling with his head lamp high up on the mountain. Everybody in camp saw him, and they all came to our tents, because they knew we were the only team in any position to carry out a rescue.

Gradually Nepali operators are taking over from western operators on Everest. This would not be a bad thing on its own, but the complete lack of regulation means that there is nothing to stop the unethical companies from operating. They can employ inexperienced Sherpas if they like and pay them low salaries. They can take money from clients with little or no experience – people who dream of climbing Everest but have no idea what it takes and are attracted by price alone. Clients of Nepali operators have little recourse if things go wrong; but clients of western operators are better protected by industry regulation and can hold their operator to account.

This trend is set to continue, and it's likely to get worse. I have written at length about the role of Nepal's government in all of this. There is no sign of things changing there, and it's time for me to stop going down that road.

At the start of this article I said that there were two sides to this issue. I've talked about one of them, but what about the other?

I feel that in some ways the western operators only have themselves to blame. A South American operator laments that it's impossible to convince clients to pay $65,000 for an expedition when other operators are offering trips for $28,000 or less. He is quite right, but I wonder if he has thought of lowering his prices. The figure of $65,000 for an

Everest expedition is one you see quoted all over the place. Why? I don't know, because it's arbitrary. You can climb Everest for a range of prices from $28,000 all the way up to a staggering $85,000. Sometimes the price corresponds to the level of service, but not always.

In 2012 I climbed Everest for $40,000 with Altitude Junkies. The level of service was everything I needed and more, but not too much more. I didn't pay for a western guide because I didn't need one. I paid for a personal Sherpa on summit day, but not for the rest of my climb. I paid for oxygen because I felt I needed it. Having an internet connection is not a necessity for me. I can keep notes and write about it when I get back. As for a base camp cinema system – well, really? I have a Kindle.

If you're an experienced climber who has climbed widely on alpine peaks and have $65,000 to spend on an Everest expedition, I highly recommend that you don't. Instead spend the first $20,000 on a commercial expedition to another 8,000m peak and $40,000 on a mid-range Everest expedition. By the time you've summited another 8,000er you may realise that you don't need to hire an expensive western guide to lead you up a line of fixed ropes – you can do that unsupervised. You will probably find that the western guide you've paid for isn't helping you, anyway, but instead is assisting other less experienced clients. You may even find yourself helping the guide if he or she could use a hand with other clients. A personal Sherpa on summit day, however, when you're pushing beyond your limits in the death zone, is money well spent – and may just save your life. An experienced expedition leader is also priceless. With such a leader, you can benefit from wise decision-making, take advice when you need it, but be a little more self-sufficient during the actual climbing.

If you're not an experienced climber and you're likely to

need more help if you tackle Everest, think very carefully about whether you're ready. A few more big peaks under your belt will put you in a much better position. The trouble with many western operators is that over the years they've gradually given their clients more and more luxuries on the mountain. This in turn has attracted clients less and less inclined (or able) to deal with the hardship. This has fooled the operators into believing that luxuries are necessities. More luxuries in turn mean higher prices, and this in turn means a smaller pool of people able to afford it.

Contrary to what they may tell you, western operators have lowered their standards when it comes to accepting clients for their expeditions. This is not surprising. As prices rise the pool of clients gets smaller, and instead of expanding the pool by lowering prices, operators have expanded it by taking less experienced clients.

The high-end western operators also have something of an image problem. Even if they can afford it, many competent climbers find the idea of hand-holding and luxuries off-putting. They might find commercial expeditions rewarding, but they feel that such trips are not for them. The commercial operators need to be reaching out to these people. For example, there is a niche for an operator to run expeditions providing advice and logistical support to people who are already competent climbers at lower altitudes, but lack experience above 8,000m. Competent, experienced climbers who are humble enough would make good commercial clients – and would also help to restore Everest's reputation.

Operators who believe $65,000 for a luxury expedition is the only way to climb Everest deserve to lose business. Times are changing and they need to diversify.

Not everyone is doing it wrong. I've mentioned Altitude Junkies as one example of a western operator with a different business model. There are other western operators with high standards who offer varying service levels to climbers depending on their needs. More experienced climbers can book a cheaper expedition with fewer services. There are also Nepali operators who offer cheaper expeditions than western operators, but employ experienced Sherpas and pay them well. There are still a few ethical options for those who can't afford $65,000 for an expedition.

Finally, on a lighter note, there is a lot of misinformation about the costs of climbing Everest, and it confuses people. They assume that we are all wealthy CEOs when we are just ordinary folk like them. One respondent on Twitter told me that I could afford it because I'm a professional climber, which nearly made me choke on my caviar. I'm grateful to him for bestowing such lavish praise, but if you've seen me climb you will know this is a bit like describing Glenn Hoddle as a professional singer. I'm neither a professional climber nor super rich. I did manage to pay for all my expeditions out of my own pocket, but I just do an ordinary day job like anyone else. It took me ten years, though, and I spent nearly all my savings on following the dream.

If you want to know how I did it then my book *Seven Steps from Snowdon to Everest* will not only persuade you that Everest is not just for the super rich, but it will hopefully entertain you too.

SHERPA HOSPITALITY AS A CURE FOR FROSTBITE

*The black limestone of Everest's summit
peeps over the West Shoulder.*

19
IN MEMORY OF CHONGBA SHERPA OF TATE, A HIGH-ALTITUDE SUPERSTAR

9 May 2018

> When I call out Chongba's name a cheerful older man steps forward, radiating warmth, and we shake hands. I'm pleased. All the Sherpas are strong, but I prefer the older guys ... who are wise as well as tough – an essential quality on big mountains.[53]

These were the words I wrote in *The Manaslu Adventure* about my first meeting with Chongba Sherpa.

Little did I know, as I re-edited the book last month, that Chongba passed away last year after a short battle with cancer. He left behind a wife and five children, two of whom are still of school age.

As we shared a tent on Manaslu in 2011, he told me his climbing record: Everest 12 times, Dhaulagiri, Cho Oyu, Kangchenjunga, Baruntse, Pumori, and Annapurna IV. He was to climb Everest at least three more times.

Because many Sherpas share the same name, it's not always easy to tell their achievements apart. This is complicated by the fact that spellings aren't always consistent. Sherpas are often described by the village they are from, though many Sherpas from the same village share names too. Chongba was from the village of Tate (pronounced *ta-tay*), across the Dudh Kosi Valley from Lukla in the Khumbu region of Nepal. The Himalayan Database lists him 27 times as Changba Nurbu Sherpa or Chhongba Nuru Sherpa, born in 1964.[54]

Here is a short summary of his climbing record. As you can see, his success rate was impressive. Interestingly, he undertook more expeditions to Everest than all the other mountains in Nepal put together.

Peak	Expeditions	Summits
Ama Dablam (6,812m)	3	2
Annapurna IV (7,525m)	1	1
Baruntse (7,152m)	1	1
Cho Oyu (8,201m)	2	1
Dhaulagiri (8,167m)	1	1
Everest (8,848m)	14	11
Manaslu (8,163m)	4	3
Pumori (7,161m)	1	1

Although this doesn't quite tally with what Chongba told me, it's pretty close, and I wouldn't dare take issue with the facts of the legendary Elizabeth Hawley. The Himalayan Database lists two other Chhongbas of a similar age and from the same part of the Khumbu region.

Chongba's first expedition was a successful ascent of Annapurna IV with an Indonesian team in 1990, when he was 26. His first 8,000m peak was Dhaulagiri with a Japanese team later the same year. His first Everest summit

IN MEMORY OF CHONGBA SHERPA OF TATE

was in 1999 with a Canadian team.

According to the Himalayan Database, his three Everest expeditions where he didn't reach the summit were with a US team in 2009 (8,700m due to fatigue), a US team in 2010 (no summit bid) and a Norwegian team in 2015 (no summit bid).

His last Everest summit was in 2016 with the UAE Armed Forces, and his final expedition was to Manaslu with a Chinese expedition in September 2016, when he reached the foresummit less than a year before his untimely death.

Chongba was my climbing Sherpa on both Manaslu in 2011 and Everest in 2012, when we reached both summits. I was also due to climb with him on Lhotse in 2014; this expedition was cut short by a strike. Chongba didn't speak much English, but it was enough for us to communicate. I remember him as quiet and attentive, radiating warmth and wisdom. He was also a devout Buddhist, I believe, in common with many Sherpas of his generation. He was proud of his climbing record. At the time I climbed with him, he had neither reached the summit of Manaslu, nor Everest from the Tibetan side, and he was as keen to get to the top as I was.

On Manaslu I remember him fiddling with my oxygen apparatus when I was slow leaving from our high camp. I didn't know that he had turned the flow rate up to four litres a minute. I went like the clappers for the next few minutes. Chongba was climbing without supplementary oxygen, and he struggled to keep up with me. At our next rest stop, he secretly turned it back down to two litres per minute. I struggled from then on, but he was now able to keep pace without difficulty.

Later in the day I descended slowly and had not reached camp when nightfall came. Chongba was safely back in Camp 2 by then, but he climbed back up with a bottle of orange juice to meet me and help me down again with my pack.

On Everest he never left my side for 18 hours as I completed my epic summit day. I was totally exhausted and in danger of falling asleep at every stop – a scenario in which many people have died on Everest by dropping into a sleep from which they never wake. Although I eventually made it back to camp under my own steam, Chongba's constant presence kept me going through those long hours. I knew that I needed to survive for his sake as much as my own.

Nowadays, the media is much more aware and supportive of Sherpa climbing achievements than they were a few years ago. Sherpa climbing fatalities are often as well publicised as those of western climbers. But we rarely hear about the Sherpas who pass away quietly.

I only learned of Chongba's death last month when I was in Kathmandu, eight months after it happened. I might not have done so had Phil Crampton of Altitude Junkies not remembered our partnership and let me know as soon as he heard the news himself. Chongba had worked with Phil for a number of years, though not recently, and Phil had only found out about his death by chance.

I don't know how prevalent cancer is among Sherpas, but I know of at least one other climbing Sherpa who passed away from cancer prematurely. Many Sherpa families still cook over open wood fires and their homes can be smoky places. Given what world-class athletes they are, you would also be surprised how many climbing Sherpas smoke cigarettes.

Chongba's death may not be attributable to either of these causes, but he was only 53 years old and has gone much too soon. His 14 Everest ascents (if indeed it was 14) puts him in a high-altitude elite.

I will never forget him and what he did for me. If you too

IN MEMORY OF CHONGBA SHERPA OF TATE

have been lucky enough to climb an 8,000m peak with Sherpa support, or are indebted to local staff for the trip of a lifetime, then please join me in taking a moment to remember those who helped us achieve our dreams.

Chongba Sherpa of Tate.

20
NIRMAL PURJA'S ASCENT OF ALL FOURTEEN 8,000M PEAKS: WHY IS IT CONTROVERSIAL?

6 November 2019

Every so often a story emerges in the world of mountaineering that is so big that it makes it into the popular press alongside stories about Brexit, Brexit and even Brexit. Last week was one of those weeks.

A Nepali climber and former soldier in the Gurkha regiment and Special Boat Service (SBS) of the British Army called Nirmal Purja completed his quest to climb all 14 of the world's 8,000m peaks in the staggeringly quick time of 189 days. He called his challenge Project Possible, and it was staggering because the previous record for climbing all 14 in the shortest time – held by the Korean climber Kim Chang-Ho – was 7 years and 10 months. By some people's reckoning, Nirmal Purja therefore beat it by 7 years and 3½ months.[55]

The mainstream press were unanimous in their praise. 'Nepali man shatters speed record for scaling the world's tallest mountains to "show human capacity",' *The Washington Post* headlined.[56]

'I don't think we will see it again in our lifetime,' *The New York Times* said, quoting his sponsor.[57]

The BBC pointed out that he not only achieved a record, but he stopped his climbs to save people's lives along the way. 'During his climbs, he rescued four other climbers – three of whom he called "suicide missions" – and has, in his own words, "bled from every angle",' their article said.[58]

The Great Outdoors (TGO) magazine even nominated his team for the Extra Mile Award alongside fundraisers, mountain rescue workers, campaigners and volunteers who have spent whole lifetimes promoting the great outdoors. The Project Possible team were cited for 'willingly risking their lives and putting their world-record project on hold to make multiple life-saving rescue attempts on various 8,000m mountains'.[59]

On the face of it, this was a straightforward story of someone smashing a record to smithereens and doing some good as they went along. But if you dig a little deeper, there is another side to it. Alongside the unqualified praise, Nirmal Purja's achievement has attracted fierce criticism.

Leading the charge were British and Polish mountaineers. Krzysztof Wielicki, the first man to climb Everest in winter, described it as a performance and organisational feat without much importance.[60] Stephen Venables, the first Briton to climb Everest without supplementary oxygen, said that 'it isn't exactly alpinism as I understand it'. He went on to say that although Nirmal Purja was fit and determined, most climbers are excited by the creativity and artistry of an unknown route rather than by speed records.'[61]

Meanwhile, Sir Chris Bonington also waded in. Sir Chris is best known for organising the siege-style expeditions that made the first ascents of the south face of Annapurna and south-west face of Everest, but he is more highly regarded among elite mountaineers for his lighter, exploratory expeditions. Sir Chris said (somewhat paradoxically) that while it was extraordinary, it wasn't a major event. He even said that it wasn't mountaineering because real mountaineering is exploratory.[62]

These men are being churlish, surely – why do they have such a problem with what Nirmal Purja did?

At the root of the controversy is an argument about style. Within the broad church of mountaineering is a smaller subset of climbers, known as alpinists, who like to climb in a certain way. Alpinists travel fast and light, carrying all their equipment with them in a single push. They eschew support from anyone other than their immediate climbing partners, and set great store in a more exploratory style of mountaineering, climbing hard technical routes that have never been climbed before.

Nirmal Purja completed his ascents in a very different style. Helicopters took him from base camp to base camp on each peak. He arrived during peak climbing season (if you'll excuse the pun) when routes had been pre-prepared with fixed ropes for those on commercial expeditions. He chose the easiest and fastest standard routes on each peak. He also committed the cardinal sin (in the eyes of alpinists) of using supplementary oxygen. This reduces many of the difficulties presented by extreme altitude, and many alpinists consider it cheating.

Are these criticisms valid? Well, if you ask me, this is the age-old problem of a certain group of people being unable to look at things from outside their bubble. It's not that they are wrong, it's just that they are judging by a different set of criteria. To put it another way, they are comparing steak with bananas.

Mountaineering means many things to many people. Most people don't care about such esoteric things as clipping into a fixed rope or treading the same route as other people, or the means of transport between each peak. Nirmal Purja never made any pretence about completing the challenge in alpine style. In an interview with ExplorersWeb, he was unapologetic about his use of oxygen. He explained that he had to consider the project as a whole: the weather, the features of the mountain, the conditions, and his need to get back down and reach the next mountain. 'You can always go again without oxygen if that is what is so important,' he concluded.[63]

It may not have been much of an achievement for those who consider the rules of alpinism as sacrosanct, but it was undeniably an achievement in other ways.

Most obviously, it was inconceivably quick. Nirmal Purja titled his challenge Project Possible for a good reason. When he first announced it, before he had climbed a single peak, most people, me included, considered it ridiculous. And for most people, it would be.

But not Nirmal Purja. He believed it was possible, and he had it well planned. First of all, there was the cost and the logistics. In this, he had the support of controversial Nepali operator Seven Summit Treks, specialists in organising expeditions to the 8,000m peaks.

Seven Summit Treks already had commercial expeditions running to many of the peaks that Nirmal Purja was climbing, including Annapurna, Kangchenjunga, Everest, K2 and Manaslu. There would already be base camps and fixed routes in place when he arrived. They have their own fleet of helicopters. They could ferry him between the peaks, and he could just turn up and climb.

Nirmal Purja has been generous in his praise of those who have supported him. In the same way that a Tour de France winner needs a team of support riders (domestiques) to keep them in the lead, he needed other climbers around him. These included 30-year-old Mingma David Sherpa, who climbed nine peaks above 8,000m with the Project Possible team this year, and Gesman Tamang, who climbed seven.

'United we conquer! Here is to The A-team: Mingma David Sherpa, Gesman Tamang, Galjen Sherpa, Lakpa Dendi Sherpa and Halung Dorchi Sherpa ... Together we have been through so much,' he posted on Facebook after his ascent of Shishapangma.[64]

There were other barriers that are not so easy to overcome. Climbing an 8,000m peak takes a lot out of you. Most people need days – sometimes even weeks – to recover from an ascent. But Nirmal Purja ticked the peaks off so quickly that he barely had time for a snack, let alone a good rest.

For example, he reached the summit of Dhaulagiri in western Nepal on 12 May, descended 3,000m to base camp, caught a helicopter to Kangchenjunga in the far east of Nepal, then climbed another 3,000m to the summit, reaching it on 15 May. He climbed Everest and Lhotse (joined by Everest's South Col) on the same day (22 May), descended 3,000m to Everest Base Camp, caught a helicopter to Makalu Base Camp, then climbed up to the summit of Makalu on 24 May. How on earth he recovered between these climbs, I have no idea.

Then there are the weather and conditions; showstoppers include high winds, extreme cold, and a surfeit of snow creating avalanche risks. To climb an 8,000m peak you have to be lucky with the weather. It's perfectly normal to spend weeks on an 8,000m peak without getting a suitable weather window.

How on earth could Nirmal Purja hope to have favourable conditions on all 14 peaks? The answer lay in the very speed that was the defining feature of his challenge. In short, he made his own luck. Because he climbed so quickly, he was able to take advantage of tiny weather windows that would be too short for most people. He only needed a few hours of good weather to sprint up and come back down again.

His supreme confidence also played to his advantage. For example, this year on K2 it was looking like another one of those seasons when nobody would reach the summit. Teams had been there for weeks waiting for a suitable window. The season was winding down and many climbers had already gone home. Then Nirmal Purja and the Project Possible team arrived. There was no way they were going to let the mountain defeat them. They blazed a trail to the top, and many other climbers who had been waiting there for weeks reached the summit in their wake.

There is another way that Nirmal Purja has been groundbreaking. He has shown what a Nepali climber can do when they have the support and the sponsorship that better-known western climbers are able to attract.

I have repeatedly written about how Sherpa mountaineers are in a different league when it comes to climbing at extreme altitude. Although Nirmal Purja isn't actually a Sherpa (he's a Magar), I believe that many other Sherpa climbers could do what he has done were they to have a similar level of support. But they haven't. The difference is that Nirmal Purja has the superstar status that has enabled him to be the first. Hopefully he has forged a path that will enable other Nepali climbers to achieve the recognition they deserve.

Some alpinists have been more generous and balanced about Nirmal Purja's achievement. These include two great Italian climbers: Reinhold Messner, the first man to climb all fourteen 8,000ers, and Simone Moro, who was the first to make winter ascents on four 8,000ers.

Simone Moro said that he could think of fewer than ten people who would be capable of repeating Nirmal Purja's achievement using the same means. Messner agreed that while Nirmal Purja's style is completely different to Jerzy Kukuczka's (the second man to climb all 14, who completed a new route or a first winter ascent on every single one), Purja did not set out to better this achievement. He had never hidden his use of oxygen and helicopters. Instead of moaning about his use of oxygen, Messner suggested that alpinists should instead rise to the challenge by trying to repeat the achievement without oxygen.[65]

But there are other sides to this story too. In setting such store in the style by which Nirmal Purja achieved his goal, other more genuinely controversial factors are in danger of being forgotten.

One of his chief sponsors, Seven Summit Treks, have been embroiled in controversy in the last year. Helicopter rescue fraud is currently a big story in Nepal. Tour operators and hospitals have been accused of carrying out unnecessary 'rescues' of foreign tourists and billing insurance companies for the helicopter evacuation and medical fees. Whether Seven Summit Treks stand guilty is not proven, but their practice of using their own fleet of helicopters to rescue their own clients has been described as a conflict of interests by US insurer Global Rescue.[66] On Annapurna, Nirmal Purja became caught up in this story when one of Seven Summit Treks' clients went missing on the mountain. Although it was their client, the operator wouldn't instigate a rescue until his insurer, Global Rescue, agreed to cover the cost. Although the climber was eventually found and brought down by Nirmal Purja and other climbers, he subsequently died in hospital. A very public feud followed. Nirmal Purja unwisely waded in by making critical comments about Global Rescue.[67]

NIRMAL PURJA'S ASCENT OF ALL FOURTEEN 8,000M PEAKS

The manner in which rescues have been used as publicity by the Project Possible team is something many people consider distasteful. Rescues happen regularly on the busier 8,000m peaks. These are usually coordinated by the larger expedition companies in cooperation with each other. While some operators do publicise these incidents if rescues are successful and they feel the victims need to be called out, many operators do not publicise them out of respect. While credit may be due, it is more dignified to keep quiet about rescues and let others do the talking.

On Everest, Nirmal Purja unwittingly instigated a much bigger media storm by taking *that* photo of a queue of climbers on the Hillary Step. The photo went viral, appearing in every media publication from Kathmandu to Timbuktu and once again Everest was in the headlines for all the wrong reasons. The same old stories buzzed around the internet. Everest has become too easy, overrun by tourists who don't know how to put on a pair of crampons.

Lost in these stories was the fact that Nirmal Purja's sponsor Seven Summit Treks has contributed to the trend of operators providing cheap trips with low levels of support and accepting clients without the necessary mountaineering experience. Seven of their clients died on the 8,000m peaks this spring season. Instead of being ashamed of this statistic their owner was quoted as saying that clients 'know they have a 50 per cent chance of returning safely and a 50 per cent chance of dying or being rescued'.[68]

More recently, questions have arisen about whether he reached the true summit of Manaslu – a mountain notorious for having a series of summits, some easier to reach than others. Not every climber is diligent about checking which summit they reach.

This year, ExplorersWeb reported that most people who climbed Manaslu didn't reach the true summit, and Nirmal

Purja may have been among them.⁶⁹ If this turns out to be true, then he could join the short list of people whose ascents of all 14 are disputed because one summit is in doubt.⁷⁰ For most people, stopping a few metres short doesn't make too much difference, but the argument is that those claiming records have to be more precise.

While Nirmal Purja's record is not currently in dispute, there are still many details about his climbs that are sketchy. The Project Possible website is light on detail, and while he has posted many verifiable summit photos and snippets of information to Facebook, these do not contain full trip reports of each ascent.⁷¹ Hopefully these details will emerge in time. When they do, the importance of his achievement can be more easily assessed.

However you choose to judge this feat, and whatever you want to call it – mountaineering, speed climbing, high-altitude peak bagging, or something completely different – there is no doubt that it has been an extraordinary achievement. It was a feat that nobody considered remotely possible, but he did it.

He has raised the bar for something, whatever that may be, and don't be surprised if he does something else to silence his critics. He has hinted about attempting K2 in winter, the last of the 8,000m peaks yet to have a winter ascent. If he manages that then it would shut a few more people up.

21
IS THE FIRST WINTER ASCENT OF K2 A TURNING POINT FOR SHERPA MOUNTAINEERS?

27 January 2021

It's not often that the ascent of an 8,000m peak makes international news headlines, but earlier this month something special happened.

At 5pm Pakistan time on 16 January 2021, a team of ten climbers stood on the summit of K2 (8,611m), the world's second-highest mountain, believed by many to be the hardest of the world's fourteen 8,000m peaks.

There were a number of reasons why this climb was special (notwithstanding the fact that it had been accomplished amid a global pandemic).

It was the first time K2 had been climbed in winter, a season when storms, snowfall, reduced daylight and extreme cold make Himalayan climbing impossible for all but the hardiest mountaineers. It was the last remaining 8,000m peak to be climbed in winter.

The expedition took three weeks from start to finish, about half the length of a standard 8,000m peak expedition – and considerably less than most winter expeditions, when teams regularly spend two or three months waiting for suitable conditions.

The expedition nearly ended a week earlier when several climbers lost tents and equipment in a storm at Camp 2. They took advantage of a tiny weather window, with a single windless summit day. At Camp 3, winds were so strong that several climbers chose to shelter in a crevasse instead of a tent.

More remarkably, it was a true team effort. The climbers congregated 10m below the summit to wait for slower members, so that they could all reach the summit together: almost unheard of on an 8,000m peak, where climbers need to get up and down as quickly as possible.

But the most notable factor is that all of the climbers were from Nepal, and, except for Nirmal 'Nims' Purja, a Magar, they were all Sherpas (and Nims, the only one of the ten to climb without bottled oxygen, is no doubt considered an honorary Sherpa).

But before I tell you why this is important, here are their names, which deserve to be emblazoned in gold along Durbar Marg, the avenue in Kathmandu leading to the Royal Palace.

- Nirmal Purja
- Gelje Sherpa
- Mingma David Sherpa
- Mingma Tenzi Sherpa
- Dawa Temba Sherpa
- Pem Chhiri Sherpa
- Mingma Gyalje Sherpa
- Kili Pemba Sherpa
- Dawa Tenjing Sherpa
- Sona Sherpa

IS THE FIRST WINTER ASCENT OF K2 A TURNING POINT?

The reason this particular ascent is significant is because Sherpas have played an integral part in the history of the 8,000m peaks, but, aside from Tenzing Norgay, who made the first ascent of Everest, they have generally been the supporting cast. This time, however, they were the stars of the show and its driving force from start to finish.

Ever since the 1920s, when British teams employed Sherpas as high-altitude porters for the first Everest expeditions, through the 1930s, when British, German, American and international teams made various attempts on Everest, K2, Nanga Parbat and Kangchenjunga, and then the 1950s, when nearly all the 8,000m peaks were climbed for the first time, Sherpas have been present in the background.

As we have seen, there have been successes and near misses. Pasang Dawa Lama came within 250m of reaching the summit of K2 with Fritz Wiessner in 1939. He was the trailblazer on the first ascent of Cho Oyu with Herbert Tichy in 1954. Angtharkay was offered the chance to make the first ascent of Annapurna with Maurice Herzog and Louis Lachenal in 1950, but decided that his feet were too cold (both Herzog and Lachenal lost fingers and toes to frostbite). Gyalzen Norbu Sherpa was involved in the first ascents of two 8,000m peaks (Makalu with a French team in 1955, and Manaslu with Toshio Imanishi in 1956), an achievement that only Hermann Buhl and Kurt Diemberger share.

Then there have been the heavy costs, which have fallen hard on the shoulders of Sherpas. Seven lost their lives in an avalanche on Everest in 1922. Three died trying to save Dudley Wolfe on K2 in 1938. Six died alongside their German teammates in a storm on Nanga Parbat in 1934. Nine were killed in an avalanche on Nanga Parbat in 1937. And of course, 14 Sherpas died alongside two other Nepalis in the Khumbu Icefall in 2014.

But until this month, no Sherpa had ever made the first

winter ascent of an 8,000m peak. This may seem surprising, but winter ascents have always been the domain of alpinists, climbers who believe that mountains should only be climbed in a certain style. Their ascents have always involved small, lightweight and self-sufficient teams who reject Sherpa support on principle. It's only recently that Sherpas have been able to afford the resources and attract the sponsorship necessary to fund their own expeditions.

At the start of this year's winter K2 season, much of the attention focused on the size of base camp (some 60 climbers) and the presence of a huge commercial group from the controversial Nepali mountaineering operator Seven Summit Treks (SST).

This drew the ire of alpinists, who were concerned about the prospect of a commercial client who needed support reaching the summit first (though this was never a realistic possibility). There was quite a bit of fuss about whether the first ascent should be made without bottled oxygen.

Four teams were at base camp, poised to battle it out to be the first and (hopefully) open doors to a more lucrative climbing career. As well as the giant SST team comprising 29 Sherpas and 25 commercial clients, there was a three-man Sherpa team led by Charles Bronson-lookalike Mingma Gyalje Sherpa (known as 'Mingma G'); a six-man Nepali team led by superstar climber Nirmal 'Nims' Purja; and the only non-Nepali expedition: a three-man team led by Icelandic climber John Snorri Sigurjónsson and including Pakistani climber Mohammed Ali Sadpara, who made the first winter ascent of Nanga Parbat in 2016.

Nims had an axe to grind with those who derided his Project Possible because he had used supplementary oxygen. Again, he intended to do what nobody had done before, but this time he would do it their way.

What happened next was something that nobody

predicted. Instead of racing each other to the summit, the three Nepali teams got together and collaborated: the six members of Nims's team (Nims, Gelje, Mingma David, Mingma Tenzi, Dawa Temba and Pem Chhiri), the three members of Mingma G's team (Mingma, Kili Pemba and Dawa Tenjing) and a single member of SST (Sona).

Whether the teams discussed the strategy in advance, or whether they realised they were ten Nepalis in a race together only when they set off on their summit push, we don't yet know.[72] But the token presence of Sona suggests that it may have been planned at base camp. SST's Sherpas had responsibilities towards their 25 clients, while Nims and Mingma's teams were free men. SST had been instrumental not only in providing logistics on K2 but also for Project Possible in 2019. It would have been good diplomacy for Nims and Mingma to let SST contribute to this joint Nepali effort, but perhaps a single Sherpa was all that SST could spare.

The team were aided by an 11th Nepali: the unsung hero Krishna Bhakta Manandhar, a meteorologist in Kathmandu who predicted a day of zero winds on Saturday 16.

Then there was the extraordinary decision to wait below the summit. We don't know who waited for whom; we're not supposed to know. I could speculate that Nims, the only one not using oxygen, was a little slower than the rest, but that's just speculation. People talk about oxygen as though it's some magic elixir, but this depends a great deal on the amount of oxygen used. Had his teammates been climbing on 4 litres per minute, there would have been no way on earth that Nims would have been able to keep up with them. But if they were climbing on only 1 or 2 litres per minute, and burdened with 8kg of additional oxygen apparatus, then there's a good chance that Nims was nearly as strong (though a good deal colder).

In any case, it doesn't matter. By waiting for each other, they were making a statement about teamwork. No single person should take all the glory. It was a breath of fresh air and symbolic of previous first ascents that had been built on the shoulders of Sherpas.

Their climb wasn't over when they reached the summit. There have been some notable tragedies on K2 that happened on the way down. In 1986 five climbers from the UK, Poland and Austria died after waiting out a three-day storm at Camp 4 on returning from the summit. In 1995, six people including British climber Alison Hargreaves were blown off the mountain while descending to Camp 4 from the summit; and in 2008, 11 climbers of many nationalities died from falls when the fixed ropes they had been relying on for descent were severed by ice.

For those ten Nepali climbers standing on the summit of K2 at 5pm with darkness looming, history was ominous. Yet just a few hours later, they were all safely back at Camp 3 with no drama. It was a great achievement, a triumph of teamwork against the odds, and a richly deserved victory for Nepali climbers.

Again there are naysayers, but their gripes are becoming increasingly obscure, such as whether it's permissible to use fixed ropes that have been fixed by people using bottled oxygen. There have even been arguments about the benefits of 'psychological oxygen' (oxygen that is carried but not used).[73]

Russian mountaineer Denis Urubko told Italian media that oxygen is doping. He pointed out that in boxing, running, skiing or cycling, athletes who dope are greeted with contempt, while in mountaineering he claimed that they become heroes.[74] Perhaps his words have been taken out of context or something was lost in translation, but in any case this is false equivalence. These other activities are

IS THE FIRST WINTER ASCENT OF K2 A TURNING POINT?

competitive sports that require a level playing field. Every mountain is different, with a different set of conditions depending on the time of year you climb it. Air pressure even differs from day to day. Scientists have calculated that Everest's perceived altitude differs by as much as 700m depending on the weather.[75] More importantly, there are no rules, and everyone is free to climb in whatever manner works for them.

Denis made this statement a few days before the Nepali ascent; perhaps he is more magnanimous now. Of all people, he will know just how challenging this climb was for the Nepalis. He also tried to make the first winter ascent of K2 in 2015 and 2018. By reaching the summit of K2 without oxygen, Nims has not only denied him the first winter ascent of K2, but also the first winter ascent of K2 without oxygen.

The door is still open for someone to make a more lightweight ascent where no one is using oxygen and call it a first, but it would be somewhat esoteric. They could also make the first winter ascent without crampons. Some people fixate on the use of oxygen above all other artificial aids, but, speaking as someone who has used both, I can confirm that crampons are far more useful on an 8,000m peak than supplementary oxygen.

There are also signs that others are softening their stance. One vocal critic of assisted ascents, the German climber Ralf Dujmovits, appeared to grudgingly offer Nims his congratulations.[76] In fact, this ascent has provided an opportunity for more enlightened members of the climbing community to make amends. The reaction to Project Possible demonstrated how an obsession with style – a curse of the climbing world that inevitably leads to exclusion – caused a form of institutional racism. To clarify what I mean by this, institutional racism refers to inbuilt prejudices that lead to discrimination against ethnic minorities, whether that racial discrimination is intentional or not. Here was a Nepali climber who had done something no one in the climbing community had come close to achieving before, and yet he was vilified because he had used techniques common in his own subcommunity of Himalayan mountaineering. It was uncomfortable to watch heroes of the climbing world react in this way.

In the wake of MeToo and the resurgence of the Black Lives Matter movement last year, some members of the climbing community – which is overwhelmingly white and male – have been re-examining how to make their sport more inclusive. Climbing routes whose names don't belong in the 21st century are being renamed.[77] The first winter ascent of K2 has given more enlightened members a second chance to give Nepali climbers the credit they are due.

Another example of this phenomenon is on Manaslu where, even before they have climbed the mountain, two Nepali climbers attempting a winter ascent have been asked questions about the style of their climb.[78] While there may be valid reasons for asking these questions for the small community of people who care about the relative importance of different climbing styles, the optics may look different to everyone else. It is highly unlikely that the Nepali climbers have been granted the same chances in life as their European counterparts. For people outside the climbing community, this is a far more impressive and interesting aspect of the story than what equipment they use.

Those who decry the achievement of these Nepali climbers are missing the bigger picture. The climbers have not only made ascents of multiple 8,000m peaks, but multiple ascents of multiple 8,000m peaks. They have done so the hard way, carrying tents and equipment for others, going up and down each mountain multiple times, fixing ropes and carrying gear so that others can follow. This is far more work than any western climber will have to face – with or without oxygen, and regardless of the style of their ascent.

The reason these Nepali climbers on K2 have gone where other western climbers have failed is less to do with fixed ropes and oxygen, and more the fact that they are significantly stronger and more experienced at extreme altitude. They have demonstrated this countless times in the limelight of lesser men and women, but this climb has put them centre stage, and they have earned it in ways that none of their western rivals can claim.

And if scenes of the crowds and hugs that greeted them in Skardu[79] seem surreal for those of us here in the UK, where thousands are dying daily of a highly infectious virus, they emphasise one certainty: that we will be hearing a lot more about the achievements of Sherpa and Nepali mountaineers in years to come.

A few days after their ascent, Nims posted what I can only describe as one of the coolest summit videos I have ever seen. Ten Nepalis, one of whom is armed with a selfie stick, stroll to the summit of the world's most dangerous 8,000m peak, arm in arm and singing as they complete their historic first ascent.[80]

For those who care about style, that's style.

SHERPA HOSPITALITY AS A CURE FOR FROSTBITE

*K2, Pakistan, scene of an
historic moment for Sherpa mountaineers.*

22
WHY TENZING IS THE GREATEST EVEREST CLIMBER

10 April 2013

I've just been reading a listicle about the five greatest Mount Everest climbers.[81] It was probably quite an easy one to write, as four of the climbers pretty much pick themselves.

Everest without George Mallory would be like Popeye without Bluto – the fate of both are inextricably linked. Not only was he the first to explore the mountain, but he was the most determined and best known of the early climbers. His disappearance on the north-east ridge in 1924 is an important part of Everest history and continues to fascinate to this day.

As the first two men to climb the mountain and return alive in 1953, Edmund Hillary and Tenzing Norgay's names are equally linked with Everest and deserve their place on the list. In 1978, Reinhold Messner became (with Peter Habeler) the first person to climb Everest without supplementary oxygen. Messner's solo ascent across the north face in 1980 broke the mould in three ways. Not only was it oxygenless, but it was by a new route. It was also the first time anyone had climbed the world's highest mountain solo and completely unsupported. If Mallory, Hillary and Tenzing were the early pioneers who broke new ground, Messner more than anyone else took climbing Everest to a new level by doing things nobody had believed possible.

The fifth name on the list is more controversial. While Eric Shipton was one of the greatest of all mountain explorers and played an important part in the early attempts – including giving both Hillary and Tenzing their opportunity – it's arguable that climbing Everest was not his forte, and ultimately the mountain defeated him.

But if not Shipton, then who should the fifth name on the list be? If Messner was the natural successor to early pioneers like Mallory and Hillary, then Apa Sherpa – who had climbed Everest a remarkable 21 times by his retirement in 2011 – represents the legacy of Tenzing more than anyone else. The history of climbing Everest belongs to the Sherpas much more than western mountaineers. It took 10 expeditions and 29 years for Everest to be climbed successfully for the first time, and members of the public were beginning to wonder whether it ever would. Now hundreds of people reach the summit every year. If this represents 'conquest' of Everest by humans (a point we can debate) then it needs to be stressed that, of those hundreds, you will probably be able to count the number who climb it without the help of a Sherpa on only a few fingers.

Which brings me to the point of this post. If there's to be an award for the greatest of all Everest climbers, then IMHO it should go to Tenzing Norgay, because he had to work so much harder to achieve his ambition than any of the other climbers. Brought up in the village of Thame close to the Sherpa capital of Namche Bazaar in the Khumbu region of Nepal, Tenzing ran away to Darjeeling in India to make his fortune. His break came when Eric Shipton was recruiting porters for the 1935 Everest expedition, and picked Tenzing out from a crowd of young hopefuls. From early on Tenzing stood apart from his Sherpa compatriots. Not only was he one of the strongest, but he also had the ambition to climb, which others lacked. He was a good organiser and became a great leader. Western expeditions came to rely on him, and he became in demand as a sirdar who would lead by example, working hard himself and persuading others to follow.

When he made the first ascent of Everest with Hillary in 1953, it was his seventh expedition there. After the 1935 expedition with Shipton, he went on two more expeditions with the British, in 1936 and 1938. The war years were a lean period for Himalayan exploration, but Tenzing went to the North-West Frontier, in what is now Pakistan, and honed his experience working for the British Army exploring the mountainous Karakoram region. Then in 1947 he joined the Canadian Earl Denman for an illicit attempt on Everest from the north. Denman had almost no money and didn't even have a permit for Tibet, so they had to travel secretly. They had little chance of success, and risked being imprisoned, but Tenzing had become consumed by Everest like no man since Mallory.

> *Any man in his right mind would have said no. But I couldn't say no. For in my heart I needed to go, and the pull of Everest was stronger for me than any force on earth ...*
> *'Well,' I told Denman, 'we will try.'*[82]

They failed even to reach the North Col, and retreated in safety back to Darjeeling. By 1952 Tibet was closed and Everest could no longer be climbed from the north side, but at the same time Nepal had ended its political isolation, and Everest became open from the south. Tenzing joined the Swiss for two expeditions on the south side. On 28 May he reached 8,600m on the south-east ridge with Raymond Lambert, but had to turn around through a combination of bad weather and exhaustion. They were 250m short of the summit – the highest anyone had ever been. They returned in the autumn for a post-monsoon attempt, but the Lhotse Face was too dangerous to climb.

By December, Tenzing was exhausted. As sirdar he had been the link between the Nepali support staff and their Swiss employers. While he was always loyal, both sides had a tendency to think he was working for the other. He had needed to recruit the support team, ensure they were paid, and deal with dissatisfaction. He encouraged and cajoled – and did his share of load carrying – while at the same time having the responsibility of being one of the lead climbers. Despite carrying more and having to deal with the added mental stress, along with Lambert he was also the strongest climber. At the end of the year he lay in a hospital in Darjeeling with fever.

It was too much ... Two expeditions. The wind and the cold. And most of all, being two things at once: a sirdar and a climber. That was too much, both in the work and the responsibility ... I lay there, and there was only weakness in my mind and body.[83]

'This whole year you must rest and get back your health,' his wife Ang Lhamu told him.

But by now he was too much in demand from expeditions travelling to the Himalayas, and, when the letter came early in 1953 inviting him to join the British Everest expedition as sirdar, he could not say no.

There was dissatisfaction with the British employers from the start. In Kathmandu, the Sherpas were made to sleep in a shed with no toilet in the grounds of the British Embassy.

WHY TENZING IS THE GREATEST EVEREST CLIMBER

The embassy staff were angry when the Sherpas peed against the wall the following morning, but it's hard to see what the poor Sherpas were expected to do. They have many remarkable qualities, but limitless bladders isn't one of them. As they travelled through the Khumbu there were frequent threats of strikes, and two of the most vocal Sherpas walked out on Tenzing. But somehow he managed to keep the logistics running smoothly, and again he was one of the strongest climbers.

The rest is history. On 29 May he stood on the summit with Hillary, and nobody was more deserving.

When I began my own Everest summit push on 15 May last year, all of our camps, from base camp at 5,270m all the way up to Camp 3 at 8,210m, had been established for us by Sherpas, and all of our oxygen cylinders were waiting for us as we arrived. All I needed to do was carry my own personal kit and put one foot in front of the other. It was far from easy – in fact it was incredibly tough – but it was much easier than it might have been thanks to our amazing Sherpa crew. My summit day on 19 May took 18 hours, and Chongba Sherpa stayed with me throughout, making his 13th ascent. I don't know whether I would have reached the summit and returned alive had he not been there. When I published my expedition journal *The Chomolungma Diaries*, I tried my best to ensure that my gratitude to our Sherpas shone through every page.

Climbing Everest is a physical challenge rather than a technical one. You don't need to be a star rock climber or ice climber. The qualities needed are the ability to remain strong and healthy at high altitude, carry heavy loads when the air is thin, and stay determined while the inhospitable climate grinds you down. You need to be patient as 24-hour winds batter against your tent, and you need to be able to exert yourself to extreme levels while slowly starving, for it's virtually impossible to eat up there. The Sherpas are able to do all these things and remain cheerful – and they return to do it again and again.

There have been some difficult technical ascents of Everest by high-profile western climbers, but that's just showing off. For me the greatest Everest climbers are the Sherpas, and Tenzing was the greatest of them all.

Everest's north side, where Tenzing Norgay began his journey into a Sherpa legend.

ACKNOWLEDGEMENTS

Indie writing can be a lonely activity. I don't have a long list of staff at my publisher to thank for bringing this book into the outside world, but I would like to thank all of the friendly people at the Alliance of Independent Authors (ALLi) for their help, encouragement and advice on bringing a book to publication.

Brief as this book may be, it's fair to say that it's been over 10 years in the making. When I first started writing my blog, *Footsteps on the Mountain*, in 2010, I had no idea where it was going to lead. But I figured that if I could write one blog post a week, then eventually it would end up where it needed to be.

In fact, it found its direction pretty quickly. For most of that time, *Footsteps on the Mountain* has represented the voice of paying clients on commercial mountaineering expeditions. We've taken a bit of a pounding in that time, both from the media and from those who take their climbing more seriously. I've enjoyed writing it, and if commercial clients are better understood now, then the writing has also been worthwhile.

Readers have come and gone in that time. Some have commented prolifically over long periods, others have followed in silence then fluttered away. Sometimes I have even received personal messages from those more famous and talented whom I have written about, which has been a great source of encouragement. I would like to thank all of you, whoever and wherever you are.

One of the great joys of writing a blog is interaction with my readers. I have been provided with constant, immediate feedback over the course of those 10 years and this has helped to shape my writing. I would like to thank the following people for their kind comments on posts in this collection, who have been my inadvertent beta readers: Alan Arnette, Aloke Surin, Andrew Lock, Anik Basu, Ann Lorenz, Ben Clark, Bert Martin, Bev Jackson, Bob A. Schelfhout Aubertijn, Carl Nelson, Carol Fruit, Cheryl Peters, Chip Brown, Chris Waters, Christian Hirsch, Chrystabel Wragg, Cody L. Custis, Colin Wallace, David M. Schauer, Dean Albrecht, Donald Walker, Douglas Mantle, Eric Welch, Gina Day, Glenn Spencer, Grant 'Axe' Rawlinson, Greg Mills, Hugues Parasie, Jay Bhosale, Jeff Armstrong, Jochen Hemmleb, John Hughes, John Quillen, Judy Tenzing, Jyotika Negi, Kate Smith, Ken Robinson, Lakshmi Priya Pampati, Lenore Jean Jones, Leo Montejo, Lisa Gibson, Lyn McKinnon, Marguerite Sherpa, Martin Berry, Matt Smith, Medhavi Gulati, Norden Sherpa, Oleg Bartunov, Paul Hickey, Peter Reynolds, Philip Hicks, Robert Anderson, Robert Kay, Serki Lhamu Sherpa, S. S. Puri, Steve Bell, Steve Berry, Stuart Macdonald, Sujoy Das, Tad Watroba, the late Ted Atkins, Todd Elichko, Tom Briggs, Tony Campbell, Tony Mercer, Tseten Sherpa, Ulrich Friebel, Vera Guinan and Vivien Martin. If you are a prolific commenter and you don't see your name mentioned, then my apologies – that's just the luck of the posts that we chose to feature. Thank you too, and perhaps you will be listed in another collection.

Speaking of those I have written about, I can't even begin to describe my debt of gratitude to all the people – too numerous to mention in person, but many have crept into

ACKNOWLEDGEMENTS

the text – who have made my adventures a reality: the guides, porters, office staff, teahouse owners, muleteers and expedition leaders. Most of all – of course – this book is dedicated to all the climbing Sherpas who have helped me and thousands of others to reach the tops of some of the world's highest mountains.

My thanks to Andrew Brown of Design for Writers for providing another evocative cover.

This wouldn't be the book it is without the support of my editor, Alex Roddie, who has helped me with a number of books over many years. Alex is a well-respected voice in the UK outdoor community, and it means a lot to have his kind words of introduction as the foreword to this book. He helped to choose the blog posts which have made up this collection, and the cunning three-part plot structure was his idea.

Finally, I would like to thank my wonderful wife Edita, companion in so many adventures, who has endured cries of 'but I've got to write another bloody blog post this weekend' with endless patience. Life's path takes many strange twists and turns. Everest 2014 looms large in the pages of this book. It has one enduring legacy for me that I wouldn't swap for anything, for it was on that expedition that I first met Edita.

NOTES

1. Tichy, *Himalaya*, 92.
2. Somervell, *After Everest*, 73.
3. Herrligkoffer, *Nanga Parbat*, 58.
4. Shipton, *The Six Mountain-Travel Books*, 407.
5. Herzog, *Annapurna*, 150.
6. Shipton, *That Untravelled World*, 204.
7. Ibid., 97.
8. Bonington, *The Everest Years*, 37.
9. Phurba Tashi did not succeed in reaching the summit in 2014, and retired from climbing Everest after that season (for reasons that will be described later).
10. Shipton, *That Untravelled World*, 197.
11. Chatwin, *What Am I Doing Here*, 276.
12. *ExplorersWeb* <explorersweb.com/> accessed 27 September 2021.
13. *Climbing@alanarnette.com* <www.alanarnette.com/blog> accessed 27 September 2021.
14. 'Everest 2013 Expedition Dispatches', *Altitude Junkies* <www.altitudejunkies.com/dispatcheverest13.html> accessed 27 September 2021.
15. *The World's Top Motorcycle Dealer* <climbwithstarcity.blogspot.com> accessed 27 September 2021.
16. Nichols, Edita, 'Mt Everest 2013 – I arrived in

NOTES

Katmandu!', *Edita's Blog – Intotheblu* <edita.blog/2013/04/03/mt-everest-2013-i-arrived-in-katmandu> accessed 27 September 2021.

17. For example: Douglas, Ed, 'Everest conquest anniversary marred by high-altitude altercation', *The Guardian* <www.theguardian.com/world/2013/apr/29/everest-conquest-anniversary-altercation> accessed 28 September 2021, and 'Everest: Climbers Steck and Moro in fight with Sherpas', *BBC News* <www.bbc.co.uk/news/world-asia-22336540> accessed 28 September 2021.
18. Douglas, Ed, 'Into the death threat zone', *BMC* <thebmc.co.uk/into-the-death-threat-zone> accessed 28 September 2021.
19. Dixit, Kunda, 'Clash of civilisations on Everest', *Nepali Times* <www.nepalitimes.com/blogs/thebrief/2013/04/29/clash-of-civilisations-on-everest> accessed 2 May 2013.
20. Brooke, Chris, '"They tried to kill us": British photographer among trio of climbers attacked by "out-of-control mob" of Sherpas in terrifying ordeal near summit of Everest', *MailOnline* <www.dailymail.co.uk/news/article-2316109/Mount-Everest-brawl-UK-photographer-Jonathan-Griffith-climbers-attacked-Sherpas.html> accessed 28 September 2021.
21. Nelson, Dean, 'Climbers "could have been killed" in Everest brawl', *The Telegraph* <www.telegraph.co.uk/news/worldnews/asia/nepal/10025117/Climbers-could-have-been-killed-in-Everest-brawl.html> accessed 28 September 2021.
22. 'Everest: Climbers Steck and Moro in fight with Sherpas', *BBC News* <www.bbc.co.uk/news/world-asia-22336540> accessed 28 September 2021.
23. @markhorrell, *Twitter*, 28 April 2013,

twitter.com/markhorrell/status/328605994403889152, accessed 28 September 2021.
24. @Venables_S, *Twitter*, 29 April 2013, twitter.com/Venables_S/status/328822918014459904, accessed 28 September 2021.
25. Neville, Tim, 'Brawl On Everest: Ueli Steck's Story', *Outside* <www.outsideonline.com/outdoor-adventure/climbing/brawl-everest-ueli-stecks-story> accessed 28 September 2021.
26. Sherpa, Lhakpa, 'A comment on the brawl incident', *Himalayan Ascent* <himalayanascent.com/live-blog/140-a-comment-on-the-brawl-incident-05-05-13-10am-.html> accessed 30 July 2013.
27. Ibid.
28. Douglas, Ed, 'Forget the Everest brawl: the real story is how Sherpas are taking control', *The Guardian* <www.theguardian.com/world/2013/may/05/sherpa-resentment-fuelled-everest-brawl> accessed 23 August 2021.
29. Pokhrel, Rajan, 'Everest expeditions uncertain', *The Himalayan Times* <thehimalayantimes.com/fullNews.php?headline=Everest+expeditions+uncertain&NewsID=412396> accessed 26 June 2014.
30. Jagged Globe and Pasang Tenzing Sherpa parted company later that year.
31. Burlakoti, Madhu Sudan. *Press Release*. Kathmandu: Ministry of Culture, Tourism and Civil Aviation, 24 April 2014.
32. Doward, Jamie, 'Qatar World Cup: 400 Nepalese die on nation's building sites since bid won', *The Guardian* <www.theguardian.com/football/2014/feb/16/qatar-world-cup-400-deaths-nepalese> accessed 29 September 2021.
33. Horrell, Mark, '5 media myths about Everest busted',

Footsteps on the Mountain <www.markhorrell.com/blog/2012/5-media-myths-about-everest-busted> accessed 30 September 2021.

34. Gold, Tanya, 'Climbing Everest is the peak of hubris', *The Guardian* <www.theguardian.com/commentisfree/2014/apr/23/climbing-everest-peak-hubris-sherpas-tragedy> accessed 30 September 2021.
35. Adwar, Corey, 'This Year Capped The Deadliest 3-Year Period For Sherpas In Everest History', *Business Insider* <www.businessinsider.com/everest-sherpas-have-higher-death-rates-than-all-other-careers-2014-4> accessed 30 September 2021.
36. Kaphle, Anup, 'A closer look at the dangerous work that Everest's Sherpas undertake for Western climbers', *The Washington Post* <www.washingtonpost.com/blogs/worldviews/wp/2014/04/21/a-closer-look-at-the-dangerous-work-that-everests-sherpas-undertake-for-western-climbers> accessed 30 September 2021.
37. Adhikari, Deepak, 'Everest disaster prompts calls for reform', *Al Jazeera* <www.aljazeera.com/features/2014/4/23/everest-disaster-prompts-calls-for-reform> accessed 30 September 2021.
38. Lallanilla, Marc, 'What Is a Sherpa?', *Live Science* <www.livescience.com/45029-what-is-a-sherpa.html> accessed 30 September 2021.
39. Ogles, Jonah, 'Everest Deaths: How Many Sherpas Have Been Killed?', *Outside* <www.outsideonline.com/outdoor-adventure/climbing/everest-deaths-how-many-sherpas-have-been-killed> accessed 30 September 2021.
40. Schaffer, Grayson, 'The Disposable Man: A Western History of Sherpas on Everest', *Outside* <www.outsideonline.com/outdoor-adventure/climbing/disposable-man-western-history-sherpas-everest> accessed 21 September 2021.

41. '2010 Census of Fatal Occupation Injuries', *U.S. Bureau of Labor Statistics* <www.bls.gov/opub/mlr/cwc/change-to-hours-based-fatality-rates-in-the-census-of-fatal-occupational-injuries.pdf> accessed 30 September 2021.
42. Ogles, Jonah, 'Everest Deaths: How Many Sherpas Have Been Killed?', *Outside* <www.outsideonline.com/outdoor-adventure/climbing/everest-deaths-how-many-sherpas-have-been-killed> accessed 30 September 2021.
43. Schaffer, Grayson, 'The Disposable Man: A Western History of Sherpas on Everest', *Outside* <www.outsideonline.com/outdoor-adventure/climbing/disposable-man-western-history-sherpas-everest> accessed 21 September 2021.
44. 'Nepal climbers face ruin after quake', *SBS News* <www.sbs.com.au/news/nepal-climbers-face-ruin-after-quake> accessed 30 September 2021.
45. Pokhrel, Rajan, 'Sherpas denied summit certificates', *The Himalayan Times* <thehimalayantimes.com/kathmandu/sherpas-denied-summit-certificates> accessed 27 August 2021.
46. Pokhrel, Rajan, 'Nepal begins probe into Everest summit manipulation by Indian couple', *The Himalayan Times* <thehimalayantimes.com/nepal/nepal-begins-probe-into-everest-summit-manipulation-by-indian-couple> accessed 30 September 2021.
47. Mountaineering Expedition Regulation, 2059 (2002 A.D.). Kathmandu: Government of Nepal.
48. Ibid.
49. Pokhrel, Rajan, 'Exposed: Officials' lies of Himalayan proportions on Everest', *The Himalayan Times* <thehimalayantimes.com/kathmandu/nepal-officials-lies-mt-everest-expedition> accessed 27 August 2021.
50. Pokhrel, Rajan, 'Foreigners barred from Upper Mustang', *The Himalayan Times*

<thehimalayantimes.com/nepal/foreigners-barred-upper-mustang> accessed 30 September 2021.
51. 'Plunging costs fuel safety fears on the world's highest peak', *The Himalayan Times* <thehimalayantimes.com/nepal/plunging-costs-fuel-safety-fears-worlds-highest-peak> accessed 27 August 2021.
52. Nepal | Data, *The World Bank* <data.worldbank.org/country/nepal> accessed 1 October 2021.
53. Horrell, *The Manaslu Adventure*, 87.
54. *The Himalayan Database* <www.himalayandatabase.com>.
55. In reality comparisons with previous records are problematic because they were judged by different criteria. The previous holders of this record (Reinhold Messner, Jerzy Kukuczka and Kim Chang-ho) had their records measured from the date they climbed their first 8,000m peak to the date they climbed their last one. Kim Chang-ho climbed his first 8,000er, Nanga Parbat, in July 2005 and his last, Everest, in May 2013. His record was therefore 7 years and 10 months. Nirmal Purja climbed his first 8,000er, Dhaulagiri, in May 2014, and his last one, Shishapangma, in October 2019. His record is therefore 5 years and 5 months, and he beat Kim's record by 2 years and 5 months. You could also argue that the other three climbers did not set out to achieve a speed record for climbing all fourteen in the shortest possible time. They did not repeat climbs in order to shorten the margin, as Nirmal Purja did with Dhaulagiri, Everest, Lhotse and Makalu, all of which he had climbed previously and repeated during Project Possible (Messner's record could also be shortened by two years if we excluded his first 8,000er, Nanga Parbat, which he later repeated). More properly, therefore, Nirmal Purja's record should be considered a new benchmark, albeit one that is going to be very hard for

anyone to improve upon.
56. Boren, Cindy, 'Nepali man shatters speed record for scaling the world's tallest mountains "to show human capacity"', *The Washington Post* <www.washingtonpost.com/sports/2019/10/29/nepal-man-shatters-speed-record-scaling-worlds-tallest-mountains-show-human-capacity> accessed 1 October 2021.
57. Specia, Megan, 'World's 14 Highest Peaks in 6 Months: Nepali Smashes Climbing Record', *The New York Times* <www.nytimes.com/2019/10/29/world/asia/nirmal-purja-record-climber.html> accessed 1 October.
58. 'Nirmal Purja: Ex-soldier climbs 14 highest mountains in six months', *BBC News* <www.bbc.co.uk/news/world-asia-50217376> 1 October 2021.
59. 'Shortlists announced for The Great Outdoors Reader Awards 2019', *The Great Outdoors (TGO)* <www.tgomagazine.co.uk/news/shortlists-announced-for-the-great-outdoors-awards-2019-vote-now/#theextramileaward> accessed 1 October 2021.
60. Wcisło, Renata, 'Zdobył wszystkie ośmiotysięczniki w 189 dni. Co na to polscy himalaiści?', *Radio Zachód* <www.zachod.pl/146602/zdobyl-wszystkie-osmiotysieczniki-w-189-dni-co-na-to-polscy-himalaisci> accessed 1 October 2021.
61. Dhillon, Amrit, 'Nirmal Purja's mountain record greeted by fit of pique', *The Times* <www.thetimes.co.uk/article/now-im-eating-humble-pie-admits-british-peak-record-holder-kenton-cool-xfrbqjxw3> accessed 1 October 2021.
62. Ibid.
63. Routen, Ash, 'Exclusive Interview: Nirmal Purja', *ExplorersWeb* <explorersweb.com/2019/08/27/exclusive-interview-nirmal-purja> accessed 1 October 2021.
64. NimsPurja, *Facebook*, 30 October 2019,

NOTES

www.facebook.com/permalink.php?story_fbid=2446967682024564&id=1923099644411373, accessed 1 October 2021.
65. Routen, Ash, 'Mixed Reviews: Himalayan Climbers Assess Purja's Feat', *ExplorersWeb* <explorersweb.com/2019/11/01/mixed-reviews-himalayan-climbers-assess-purjas-feat> accessed 6 November 2019.
66. Arnette, Alan, 'Everest Rescue Scams Expose Corruption Across Nepal', *Climbing@alanarnette.com* <www.alanarnette.com/blog/2018/08/29/everest-rescue-scams-expose-corruption-across-nepal> accessed 31 August 2021.
67. Routen, Ash, 'Did Red Tape Fatally Delay the Rescue on Annapurna?', *ExplorersWeb* <explorersweb.com/2019/04/30/rescue-on-annapurna-delayed-due-to-red-tape> accessed 1 October 2021.
68. Routen, Ash, '"Death, Carnage, Chaos": Analysing the 2019 Himalayan Climbing Season', *UKClimbing* <www.ukclimbing.com/articles/mountaineering/death_carnage_chaos_analysing_the_2019_himalayan_climbing_season-11996> accessed 1 October 2021.
69. Benavides, Angela, 'Manaslu's Can of Worms: Did Anyone at All Reach the True Summit?', *ExplorersWeb* <explorersweb.com/2019/10/25/manaslus-can-of-worms-did-anyone-at-all-reach-the-true-summit> accessed 31 August 2021.
70. Nirmal Purja is not the only climber whose achievements have come under scrutiny as a result of the Manaslu foresummit controversy. In the autumn season, Manaslu's foresummit is usually a snowy cornice hiding a short, knife-edge ridge to the main summit, which is 7m higher. Since 2008, when Manaslu became a popular peak for commercial expeditions, operators have been ending the fixed ropes a metre or

two below the foresummit, even bedecking them with prayer flags to indicate the top. This has meant that most commercial clients (including myself) have stopped short, without realising that there is a higher summit just beyond the cornice. But it's not just commercial clients who have been deceived. Statistician Eberhard Jurgalski has studied the ascents of 35 of the 44 climbers who have climbed all fourteen 8,000m peaks, and he believes that only 6 of them reached the true summit of Manaslu (see Nestler, Stefan, 'Manaslu debate: When is a summit a summit?', *Adventure Mountain with Stefan Nestler* <abenteuer-berg.de/en/manaslu-debate-when-is-a-summit-a-summit> accessed 15 October 2021). In September 2021, Mingma Gyalje Sherpa (a.k.a. 'Mingma G') of Nepali operator Imagine Nepal did what perhaps his competitors should have done years earlier, and fixed a new route to the main summit by lowering a rope down from the foresummit and traversing beneath the dangerous, corniced summit ridge.

71. *Project Possible*, <projectpossible.co.uk> accessed 5 November 2019.
72. They revealed later that they had indeed agreed the plan in advance during a meeting at base camp.
73. Benavides, Angela, 'K2: The Oxygen Controversy', *ExplorersWeb* <explorersweb.com/2021/01/08/k2-the-oxygen-controversy> accessed 1 October 2021.
74. Filippini, Alessandro, 'Urubko: "L'ossigeno è il doping dell'alpinismo"', *Alpinisti e Montagne* <alpinistiemontagne.gazzetta.it/2021/01/12/urubko-lossigeno-e-il-doping-dellalpinismo> accessed 1 October 2021.
75. Matthews, Tom et al., 'Into Thick(er) Air? Oxygen Availability at Humans' Physiological Frontier on Mount Everest', *ScienceDirect* <www.sciencedirect.com/

science/article/pii/S2589004220309159> accessed 1 October 2021.
76. Nestler, Stefan, 'Dujmovits on Purja's K2 winter success without breathing mask: "Nine witnesses at the summit"', *Adventure Mountain with Stefan Nestler* <abenteuer-berg.de/en/dujmovits-on-purjas-k2-winter-success-without-breathing-mask-nine-witnesses-at-the-summit> accessed 1 October 2021.
77. 'de Bruijn, Bonnie, 'Controversy Over Sexist Route Names: Really?', *Gripped* <gripped.com/profiles/controversy-over-sexist-route-names-really> accessed 1 October 2021.
78. Benavides, Angela, 'Nepalis on Manaslu: Yes, We're Going Alpine Style', *ExplorersWeb* <explorersweb.com/2021/01/25/nepalis-on-manaslu-yes-were-going-alpine-style/> accessed 1 October 2021.
79. @nimsdai, *Twitter*, 23 January 2021, twitter.com/nimsdai/status/1352925937793380352, accessed 1 October 2021.
80. @nimsdai, *Twitter*, 24 January 2021, twitter.com/nimsdai/status/1353269945254162432, accessed 1 October 2021.
81. Green, Stewart, 'The Story of the 5 Greatest Mount Everest Climbers', *tripsavvy* <www.tripsavvy.com/greatest-mount-everest-climbers-755318> accessed 1 October 2021.
82. Norgay, *Tiger of the Snows*, 82.
83. Ibid., 201.

BIBLIOGRAPHY

Bonington, Chris. *The Climbers: A History of Mountaineering.* London: Hodder and Stoughton, 1992.

Bonington, Chris. *Annapurna South Face.* New Delhi: Book Faith India, 1997.

Bonington, Chris. *The Everest Years: A Climber's Life.* Coronet Books, 1987.

Braham, Trevor, ed. *Club Proceedings, 1958.* Himalayan Journal, Vol. 21, 1958

Bruce, Charles, et al. *The Assault on Mount Everest 1922.* London: Edward Arnold, 1923.

Chatwin, Bruce. *What Am I Doing Here.* London: Pan Books, 1990.

Conefrey, Mick. *Everest 1953: The Epic Story of the First Ascent.* London: Oneworld Publications, 2012.

Conefrey, Mick. *The Last Great Mountain: The First Ascent of Kangchenjunga.* A Mick Conefrey Book, 2020.

Davis, Wade. *Into The Silence: The Great War, Mallory and the Conquest of Everest.* London: Random House, 2011.

Douglas, Ed. *Tenzing: Hero of Everest.* Washington, DC: National Geographic Society, 2003.

Farquhar, Francis, ed. *Various Notes.* American Alpine Journal, Vol. 9, No. 2, 1955.

Gillman, Peter, ed. *Everest: Eighty years of triumph and tragedy.* London: Little, Brown and Co, 2001.

BIBLIOGRAPHY

Gregson, Jonathan. *Blood Against the Snows: The Tragic Story of Nepal's Royal Dynasty*. New Delhi: HarperCollins, 2002.

Herrligkoffer, Karl M. *Nanga Parbat*. New York: Alfred A. Knopf, 1954.

Herzog, Maurice. *Annapurna: The First Conquest of an 8000-Metre Peak*. Jonathan Cape, 1952. Pimlico ed., London: Pimlico, 1997.

Hillary, Edmund. *View from the Summit*. London: Corgi, 2000.

Horrell, Mark. *Seven Steps from Snowdon to Everest: A hill walker's journey to the top of the world*. Mountain Footsteps Press, 2015.

Horrell, Mark. *The Chomolungma Diaries: Climbing Mount Everest with a commercial expedition*. Mountain Footsteps Press, 2016.

Horrell, Mark. *The Everest Politics Show: Sorrow and strife on the world's highest mountain*. Mountain Footsteps Press, 2017.

Horrell, Mark. *Thieves, Liars and Mountaineers: On the 8,000m peak circus in Pakistan*. Mountain Footsteps Press, 2017.

Horrell, Mark. *The Manaslu Adventure: Three hapless friends try to climb a big mountain*. Mountain Footsteps Press, 2018.

Hunt, John. *The Ascent of Everest*. London: Hodder and Stoughton, 1953.

Imanishi, Toshio. *The First Assault Party*. The Mountain World, 1958/59, 180-190, 1958.

Isserman, Maurice, and Stewart Weaver. *Fallen Giants: A History of Himalayan Mountaineering from the Age of Empire to the Age of Extremes*. New Haven: Yale, 2008.

Krakauer, Jon. *Into Thin Air: A Personal Account of the Mount Everest Disaster*. London: Pan Books, 1998.

Mason, Kenneth. *Abode of Snow: A History of Himalayan*

Exploration and Mountaineering from Earliest Times to the Ascent of Everest. Rupert Hart-Davis, 1955. Diadem ed., London: Diadem Books, 1987.

Messner, Reinhold. *All 14 Eight-Thousanders*. Marlborough: Crowood Press, 1988.

Messner, Reinhold. *The Crystal Horizon: Everest - The First Solo Ascent*. Marlborough: Crowood Press, 1989.

Messner, Reinhold. *My Quest for the Yeti: Confronting the Himalayas' Deepest Mystery*. London: Pan Books, 2001.

Morris, Jan. *Coronation Everest*. London: Faber and Faber, 1958. Paperback ed., London: Faber and Faber, 2003.

Murray, W. H. *The Reconnaissance of Mount Everest, 1951*. Alpine Journal, Vol. 58, No. 285, November 1952.

Neale, Jonathan. *Tigers of the Snow*. London: Abacus, 2003.

Newby, Eric. *Great Ascents: A Narrative History of Mountaineering*. Vancouver: Douglas David & Charles, 1977.

Ngawang Tenzin Zangbu, and Frances Klatzel. *Stories and Customs of the Sherpas*. 4th ed., Kathmandu: Mera Publications, 2000.

Norgay, Tenzing, and James Ramsey Ullman. *Tiger of the Snows: The autobiography of Tenzing of Everest*. New York: G.P. Putnam's Sons, 1955.

Norton, Edward, et al. *The Fight for Everest 1924*. Kathmandu: Pilgrims Publishing, 2002. New edition, 2015, available from Vertebrate Publishing.

Noyce, Wilfrid. *South Col: One Man's Adventure on the Ascent of Everest, 1953*. London: Heinemann, 1954. Birlinn ed., Edinburgh: Birlinn, 2003.

O'Connor, Bill. *The Trekking Peaks of Nepal*. Marlborough: The Crowood Press, 1989.

Purja, Nimsdai. *Beyond Possible: One Soldier, Fourteen Peaks – My Life in the Death Zone*. London: Hodder & Stoughton, 2020.

BIBLIOGRAPHY

Sale, Richard, and John Cleare. *On Top of the World: Climbing the World's 14 Highest Mountains.* London: HarperCollins, 2000.

Shipton, Eric. *The Six Mountain-Travel Books.* London: Baton Wicks, 1999.

Shipton, Eric. *That Untravelled World.* London: Hodder and Stoughton, 1969.

Smythe, Frank. *The Six Alpine/Himalayan Climbing Books.* London: Baton Wicks, 2000.

Somervell, Howard. *After Everest.* London: Hodder & Stoughton, 1947.

Steele, Peter. *Eric Shipton: Everest and Beyond.* London: Constable, 1998.

Tenzing, Jamling, and Broughton Coburn. *Touching My Father's Soul: In the Footsteps of Sherpa Tenzing.* London: Random House, 2002.

Tenzing, Tashi, and Judy Tenzing. *Tenzing Norgay and the Sherpas of Everest.* Camden: Ragged Mountain Press, 2001.

Tichy, Herbert. *Himalaya.* London: Robert Hale, 1971.

Tichy, Herbert. *Cho Oyu: By Favour of the Gods.* London: Methuen, 1957.

Tilman, H. W. *The Seven Mountain-Travel Books.* London: Baton Wicks, 2003.

Unsworth, Walt. *Everest.* Oxford Illustrated Press, 1989. Grafton ed., London: Grafton, 1991.

Venables, Stephen, et al. *Everest: Summit of Achievement.* 60th anniversary ed., London: Bloomsbury, 2013.

Viesturs, Ed, and David Roberts. *K2: Life and Death on the World's Most Dangerous Mountain.* New York: Broadway, 2009.

ABOUT THE AUTHOR

For many years Mark Horrell has been writing what has been described as one of the most credible Everest opinion blogs out there. He writes about trekking and mountaineering from the often silent perspective of the commercial client.

For 20 years he has been exploring the world's greater mountain ranges and keeping a diary of his travels. As a writer he strives to do for mountain history what Bill Bryson did for long-distance hiking.

Several of his expedition diaries are available from the major online bookstores. He has published two full-length books: *Seven Steps from Snowdon to Everest* (2015), about his ten-year journey from hill walker to Everest climber, and *Feet and Wheels to Chimborazo* (2019), about an expedition to cycle and climb from sea level to the furthest point from the centre of the earth.

His favourite mountaineering book is *The Ascent of Rum Doodle* by W.E. Bowman.

YOU MIGHT ALSO LIKE

Seven Steps from Snowdon to Everest
A hill walker's journey to the top of the world

As he teetered on a narrow rock ledge a yak's bellow short of the stratosphere, with a rubber mask strapped to his face, a pair of mittens the size of a sealion's flippers, and a drop of two kilometres below him, it's fair to say Mark Horrell wasn't entirely happy with the situation he found himself in.

He was an ordinary hiker who had only read books about mountaineering, and little did he know when he signed up for an organised trek in Nepal with a group of elderly ladies that ten years later he would be attempting to climb the world's highest mountain.

But as he travelled across the Himalayas, Andes, Alps and East Africa, following in the footsteps of the pioneers, he dreamed up a seven-point plan to gain the skills and experience which could turn a wild idea into reality.

Funny, incisive and heartfelt, his journey provides a refreshingly honest portrait of the joys and torments of a modern-day Everest climber.

ISBN (ebook): 978-0-9934130-1-8
ISBN (paperback): 978-0-9934130-2-5
ISBN (audiobook): 978-1-9127480-8-2

First published in 2015. A list of bookstores can be found at: www.markhorrell.com/SnowdonToEverest

YOU MIGHT ALSO LIKE

The Everest Politics Show
Sorrow and strife on the world's highest mountain

In April 2014 Mark Horrell went on a mountaineering expedition to Nepal, hoping to climb Lhotse, the fourth-highest mountain in the world, which shares a base camp and climbing route with Mount Everest.

He dreamed of following in the footsteps of Tenzing Norgay and Edmund Hillary, by climbing through the infamous ice maze of the Khumbu Icefall, and he yearned to sleep in the grand amphitheatre of Everest Base Camp, surrounded by towering peaks.

He was also intrigued by the media publicity surrounding commercial expeditions to Everest. He wanted to discover for himself whether it had become the circus that everybody described.

But when a devastating avalanche swept across the Khumbu Icefall, he got more than he bargained for. Suddenly he found himself witnessing the greatest natural disaster Everest had ever seen.

And that was just the start. Everest Sherpas came out in protest, issuing a list of demands to the Government of Nepal. What happened next left his team shocked, bewildered and fearing for their safety.

ISBN (ebook): 978-0-9934130-5-6
ISBN (paperback): 978-0-9934130-6-3

First published in 2016. A list of bookstores can be found at: www.markhorrell.com/TheEverestPoliticsShow

YOU MIGHT ALSO LIKE

The Chomolungma Diaries
Climbing Mount Everest with a Commercial Expedition

In April 2012 Mark Horrell travelled to Tibet hoping to become, if not the first person to climb Mount Everest, at least the first Karl Pilkington lookalike to do so.

He joined a mountaineering expedition which included an Australian sexagenarian, two Brits whose idea of hydration meant a box of red wine, and a New Zealander who enjoyed reminding his teammates of the perils of altitude sickness and the number of ways they might die on summit day.

The media often write about Mount Everest deaths and how easy the world's highest mountain has become to climb, but how accurately does this reflect reality?

The Chomolungma Diaries is a true story of ordinary people climbing Mount Everest with a commercial expedition, and preparing for the biggest day of their lives.

Imagine your life clipped into a narrow line of cord five miles above the earth, on the world's most terrifying ridge walk. This book will bring you just a little bit closer to that experience.

ISBN (ebook): 978-0-9934130-3-2
ISBN (paperback): 978-0-9934130-4-9
ISBN (audiobook): 978-1-9127480-9-9

Revised edition first published in 2016. A list of bookstores can be found at:
www.markhorrell.com/TheChomolungmaDiaries

CONNECT

You can join Mark's **mailing list** to keep updated:
www.markhorrell.com/mailinglist

Website and blog: www.markhorrell.com
Twitter: @markhorrell
Facebook: www.facebook.com/footstepsonthemountain
Flickr: www.flickr.com/markhorrell
YouTube: www.youtube.com/markhorrell

DID YOU ENJOY THIS BOOK?

Thank you for buying and reading this book. Word-of-mouth is crucial for any author to be successful. If you enjoyed it then please consider leaving a review. Even if it's only a couple of sentences, it would be a great help and will be appreciated enormously.

Links to this book on the main online bookstores can be found at:
www.markhorrell.com/SherpaHospitality